I0022239

GUNSMART NATION

DH BOOKS are published by,
DH Publishing Company
P.O. Box 333
Indianapolis, IN 46250

Gunsmart Nation Copyright©2020 by Dwight Bradford

All rights reserved. No part of this book may be
reproduced in any form or by any means without the
prior written consent of the Publisher.
This is a work of fiction. All events, characters, places,
and incidents are strictly a product of the author's
imagination or are used fictitiously, and any
resemblance to actual persons, living or dead is purely
coincidental.

ISBN: 978-1-7336502-4-3
Book cover design: Chalandon Walker
Publisher: DH Publishing Company

DH Books

GUNSMART NATION

Dwight B. Bradford

DEDICATION

I dedicate this book to my late sister, Delois Banks, who has always had my back. Without a doubt, I always knew I could count on Lois to be there for me with a vast array of support, no matter what my endeavor. Often times, she would bring forth great ideas as well as words of encouragement.

Lois was always willing to lend a helping hand both physically and financially. Lois was a person with a really big heart.

ACKNOWLEDGEMENTS

Many thanks to the people in my life who through their words of encouragement helped me to stay focused, and to keep moving forward.

First and foremost is my beautiful wife and best friend, Dinah Marie, who has always been there for me, praying both with me and for me. She has been so loving and understanding, as I would often render so much time to the writing of several different projects.

Thanks to my beautiful daughters, Krystle, and LaToya, who continue to offer a prayer and words of encouragement.

Janet Lynn Mason, who checks in on occasion to see how the projects are coming along and stating she's gonna keep pushing me until I get there. Thanks, Lynn, I needed that.

Greatly appreciated were the words of encouragement received from Leander Lloyd, Vincent Pearson, Freddy Kincaid, Darnell Miller, Earl Parhm, and Alexander Parhm. Conversations with these guys always gave me a fresh burst of energy.

Even with so much encouragement, there still comes a time when a writer will experience burnout. Thanks to guys like Marvin Stewart, our track team captain, and Henry Smith, our racing champion, both of whom in different ways, taught me that when the going gets tough, we go even harder.

Special thanks to Debra Hollis Smith for the many long conversations about career, prayer, and God's will.
Many thanks for the well wishes from my big sister, Janice Lloyd Lucas.

I shall never forget the words of my late uncle Ollie Lloyd, a farmer in rural Mississippi. One day we were having a conversation and he was inquiring about my plans for life.
After I'd finished revealing my goals, he first commended me for having a good honest plan. He then went on to plant a forever lasting seed into my spirit, stating that, "In this life, one can achieve just about anything he or she puts their mind to. But one thing about it, you just need to be wholehearted and keep God in it."

Lee and Michelle become advocates for gun reform following the rape and murder of a mutual friend.

Prologue

Leander Cross (Lee), a Hollywood movie producer, returns to Indianapolis (Indy) to sell the house where he once lived with his parents before moving to California.

While in town, Lee attends a neighborhood crime watch meeting. There he meets committee members Paula Gaines and Michelle Anderson. Little did they know that Lee and Michelle would later team-up and head to Washington to fight for better gun control, and to avenge the rape and murder of Michelle's best friend.

As a team, Lee and Michelle would spend a great deal of time together, as they traveled from place to place attending several different meetings, all of which pertained to gun reform. Time spent together led to developed feelings.

On the most memorable night in Indy, while the Cross Property was taped off as a crime scene, Michelle opens her doors to Lee as a kind gesture. Before this night their relationship was merely cordial, mostly about business, although unspoken feelings were mounting. They both, value their relationship as it stands, but find themselves secretly contemplating whether or not there exists a significant line between business and pleasure, and if so, do they dare cross it? If indeed there were lines, on that night, they became very blurred.

With great effort, they would continue to fight for better gun control. Their hope is that, by gaining nationwide support from several different advocacy groups, it would ultimately lead to America becoming a gun smart nation.

CHAPTER 1

Returning Home to Sell the Property

On a beautiful sunny day, in Indianapolis, in the early part of the evening, Leander Cross Jr. (Lee), drove down the street taking in the sights. Lee was born and raised in Indianapolis, and now resides in Hollywood as a prominent movie producer. He had returned home to sale the house where he'd lived with his parents before moving to California. The sale of the property would take approximately twelve weeks to complete, thus allowing plenty of time for an unsuspecting relationship to develop.

While driving along the streets of Indy, after leaving the real estate office, Lee reminisced about some of the places he'd visited while living there. Before heading to a neighborhood meeting, Lee decided to pull into a familiar station for gas just as he had done many times in the past.

At the station, there were several types of unflattering and unlawful activities taking place, which consisted of rimmed-up vehicles playing very loud obnoxious music, the passing of money and packages, weapons being displayed, people smoking marijuana, drinking, loud laughing, swearing, and young ladies hanging around dressed like hookers, jumping in and out of different vehicles. Two guys stepped out of different vehicles and faced one another. They stood approximately ten feet apart, pointing their weapons at one another. About the last thing that Lee would have expected, would be to witness a murder take place right in front of his eyes. But, surprisingly so, all of a sudden, the two guys start shouting, "Bang-bang-bang" at one another, followed by an outbreak of laughter, and on to hugging one another.

Lee thought to himself, "These people are crazy." Remembering a time when the area used to be very decent, he could only shake his head at what it had become. The whole time that Lee stood there filling his tank, not one other vehicle pulled in for gas. It seems as though, the only other patrons of the station, were more of the same, as that which was already present, when he arrived.

A few police cruisers passed by the station, but they didn't seem to give the place much thought as they just kept right on rolling. It seemed as though, cops patrolling this area had decided that, unless they receive a dispatch to the place, they don't stop. Considering the way things are these days, Lee could certainly understand, cop or no cop, at the end of the day, they want to be able to go home and enjoy their families, just like everyone else. He finished pumping his gas and left the station.

The First Neighborhood Meeting

A neighborhood meeting was already in progress when Lee arrived. He entered and found committee leader, Michelle Anderson, at the podium as she spoke to the members of the Homeowners Association (H.O.A.). Lee took a seat near the back of the room. Michelle continued saying, "for about eleven years now, I've been a part of this community. I love it here, it's home! But over the past few years, I've noticed, things have taken a turn for the worse."

While the people of the neighborhood, met on the inside, guys on the outside, who do not live in the neighborhood, came rolling through in a rimmed-up, old school vehicle.

Michelle's teenage daughter Lindsey, along with a few of her girlfriends, was walking along the sidewalk. The young ladies were spotted by the guys in the fancy car. The guy in the front passenger seat was the first to speak, "Hey, what's up ladies?" The guy in the rear passenger side took his turn to throw out a line, "Fine mamas like y'all ain't got no business walking. Hop on in and roll with us." The girls were somewhat flattered, but still, they had the good sense to decline, "No thanks, we're fine," Lindsey said. The front passenger guy responded, "You got that right, baby. Whoa!" The guys sped off, throwing out empty beer cans and other pieces of trash onto someone's nicely manicured lawn.

Meanwhile, back inside at the meeting, Michelle continued, "As chairperson, I have read your letters, I've heard your concerns… your very legitimate concerns. This brings me to the point of opening the floor to suggestions. What are we going to do about all of these senseless crimes and unflattering activities that continue to plague, not only our neighborhood but, communities abroad?"

After an extended moment of silence, Michelle asked, "Suggestions, anyone?" She summoned Paula, "How about you Paula? I remember Just the other day you mentioned that you saw a person who you felt may have been casing your home."

Paula Gaines, who happened to be Michelle's best friend, was seated about three rows back. She came to the front of the room, but elected not to take to the podium, nor did she take the microphone, as she began to speak candidly to the crowd. "Well… it all started, as Michelle mentioned, a few days ago, as I was in the checkout line at Rae's Supermarket.

You know how sometimes you can kind of feel when someone's looking at you, right? So, I looked up and noticed this guy coming into the store, and he was staring right at me as he walked by. I didn't think his stare was one of a flirtatious type, nor did it seem to be an identity question, like… where do I know you from, type of thing. Instead, it felt more like a predatory or stalking type of thing, you know? It certainly gave me the feeling that something was not quite kosher about this guy. So anyway, he walked on in and disappeared a few isles down the way. By the time I reached the cashier, and I'm standing there paying for my items, I noticed the guy as he comes back by empty-handed, to exit the store.

By the time I'd finished paying and had gone outside, I looked around to see if the suspicious guy would be out there laying wait. Relieved that I didn't see him anywhere, I got into my car and headed for home.

When I reached the traffic light where I would turn into my neighborhood, I noticed in my rearview mirror, the suspicious guy was right behind me. I turned… he turned! I turned again… he turned again! At this point, my mind starts racing and clever thinking has gone right out the window.

I pulled into my driveway and very slowly the suspicious guy drove on by, but only after getting a good long look. Well, that brought about a chilling feeling, which led me to go into my bedroom and grab my protection, if you know what I mean. So, with my little security guard in hand, I go to peep out of the window and see him slowly passing by a second time. I watched as he turned the corner onto the street leading out of the neighborhood.

From the back of my home, I can see the intersection that is the point of entry to the neighborhood. So… just to make sure he was really gone, I run to peep out the patio door. From there I watched him turn onto the main street, as he left the neighborhood.

Thank God, I've never seen or heard from that guy again. Now… I can't say for certain, that his intentions were bad. But… because of that encounter… today I stand, as should we all, much more aware of my surroundings and the circumstances thereof. Thank you!"

The people applauded as Paula took her seat. Michelle returned to the podium. "Thank you, Paula, for sharing with us. That was certainly an interesting story, with a notable take away, if I might add.

Now, if everyone would just take a look at the handout you received when you came in. On it, you'll notice a list of crimes that have occurred and continue to take place throughout our community. Also, you'll notice a list of suggestions, I've jotted down, that we might try in an effort to make our community safer. But I'd also like to hear from you. What would be your thoughts or suggestions? So please take it home, look it over, and if you have any comments or suggestions, please write them down and we'll be happy to discuss them at the next meeting, as we seek a strategy to move forward toward making our community a safer place to live. Thanks for coming out this evening and be safe out there. Meeting adjourned!"

CHAPTER

2

Lee Meets Paula

As people started to exit the neighborhood clubhouse, Lee spoke to Paula who was about to pass by him on her way out. "Hello Miss Paula," Lee said.

Paula stopped to respond. "Hello."

Lee continued, "If I may, that was quite an interesting observation you had going on there. And I certainly agree with Michelle, on the inspiring takeaway."

"Well, thank you, but I believe she said notable takeaway."

"Oh, it goes beyond notable. The end part... absolutely inspiring."

"Well... alright then," Paula said.

"However, you did make a very serious mistake.

But… you already know that."

"Yeah, I do. By the way… I don't believe we've met."

"I'm sorry, pardon my manners."

Lee extended his hand to shake as he introduced himself.

"Leander Cross, friends call me Lee."

Paula accepted his hand, "Well Mr. Cross--"

He cut her off, "Please… call me Lee. And that's Lee with an A… L-E-A… not L-E-E."

Paula responded, "Oh! Lee with an A… I see!"

He could see that she was contemplating a tactical way to respond to the A.

"What?" Lee asked.

Paula responded, "Well… you do know that, with an A… it's kind of, uh--"

He cut in, "feminine? Absolutely."

"So--?"

Knowing what her question would be, he said, "No! Absolutely not! It's just the first three letters of my name. That's all! But, to keep it simple, L-E-E will be just fine."

"Whatever you say, after all, it's your name. So… Lee with an A, are you new to the neighborhood?"

"Kind-of sort-of."

"Well, either you are, or you aren't!"

"Actually, I have returned to the neighborhood, but only for a short time, just long enough to get my dad's house sold."

"I see. So, which house are we talking about?"

"The one on the corner as you enter the neighborhood."

"As you enter the neighborhood from Michigan Rd.?"

"That's the one!"

Realizing which house Lee was talking about, Paula's mouth dropped open, "Oh yeah… Cross. You're Mr. John Lee's son… Jr.! You're the one he talks about all the time."

"In the flesh," Lee said smiling, "but, remember… friends call me Lee. Jr., is reserved only for my dad."

Paula, who had only heard of Lee but had never met him before this encounter, started to warm up to him a bit as she

7

felt as though she knew him somewhat through past conversations with his dad. Also, she couldn't help but notice he was quite a handsome guy, absolute eye candy for the ladies.

"Well then, Lee with an A... welcome back to the neighborhood."

"Thank you."

Paula continued, "since I'm just two houses down from you, I guess we'll be neighbors for however long it takes for you to get the house sold."

Lee Meets Michelle

Heading toward the exit, Michelle was stopped by Paula, who attempted to make an introduction.

"Hey, Michelle, this is--" Paula got cut off as Michelle said, "Leander."

Paula was very surprised by the fact that her best friend Michelle, with whom she shared her most personal information, had never made mention of this guy.

"So, you already know him?" Paula asked.

"Kind-of sort-of," Michelle said.

Paula repeated, as she looked at Lee, "Kind-of sort-of. Now, where have I heard that, just recently?"

There came an odd pause in the conversation.

"Okay, what am I missing here? Just how well do you guys know one another?" Paula asked.

"We haven't met formally, Michelle responded. But I've seen him around. I know that he and his parents were the first to build in this neighborhood."

Michelle said to Lee, "I understand that the unique designs throughout the home were all created by you."

"Yep. That is correct," he said.

There came another brief silence. Michelle went on to say, "I used to wonder what happened to you, that is, until your dad mentioned that you had moved to California."

"Yeah, long story there."

"Oh…" Michelle said, "Well, if you wouldn't mind sharing, I'm sure we'd love to hear it." Reaching into his inner jacket pocket, "Well, it's no wonder that they've named you chairperson," Lee said, "I see you like to keep on top of things. If it's okay, I'd be happy to tell you all about it over dinner sometime."

Thinking that the dinner invite was only for Michelle, Paula felt as though she had just been upstaged by her good friend. Lee pulled out two business cards and handed one to each of the ladies, Michelle first, then Paula as he looked at her saying, "The both of you."

Paula looked, and was, pleasantly relieved.

CHAPTER 3

Potential Buyer

People and traffic moved about, outside the office building of A-TEAM REALTY. Inside, owner Toni Bradshaw strolled through the lobby as she stopped to receive mail and messages from her assistant Karen Powell, before heading into her office.

"We have a bite on the Cross property," Karen mentioned.

"Oh! That was quick. I'd better go follow up, thanks," Toni said.

Once in her office, Toni placed the mail on her desk, took her seat and made a call to Monica Morgan, the potential buyer. At home anxiously awaiting a call from the realty company, Monica answered her phone on the very first ring, "Hello?" With the speaker on, Toni said, "Hi, I'm Toni Bradshaw with A-TEAM REALTY calling for Monica Morgan please."

"This is Monica."

"And how's your day going so far?" Toni asked.

"Just fine," Monica replied.

"Wonderful! So, I understand you've expressed an interest in one of our listings."

After speaking for a while, they set an appointment for the showing of the property, which would be the very next day. Toni instructed Karen to call and inform Mr. Cross of the time set for the showing.

At the Cross property, Lee was in the kitchen fixing a bite as he caught a news report about a teenage boy who was shot at a house party. The reporter said, "Just in, we have an update on the teenager who was shot while attending a house party last Saturday on the city's east side. Though still in the hospital in the intensive care unit, sources tell us that he is stable and expected to survive.
After taking a bullet to the head, he suffers from severe brain damage, causing paralysis to more than fifty percent of his body. Doctors fear that he may never be able to walk again, or even be able to feed himself. Alice Buckner, channel seven news."

The phone rang. Lee recognized the incoming number as being that of the real estate office. He lowered the volume on the TV. Expecting to hear the voice of Toni Bradshaw, he answered the phone, "Toni, hey, what's up?"
The caller was Karen who said, "Right office... wrong girl, it's Karen."

"Oh Karen, well, it's all good. Either way I'm happy to hear from you."

"Well, good, then you'll be even happier to know that we have a showing scheduled for tomorrow at seven pm, if that works for you."

"Sure! That will be just fine. Actually... I have a dinner engagement about that time, so yeah, you can just come on in and do your thing."

"A dinner date, huh?"

"Engagement... dinner engagement! I don't know that I would call it a date," Lee responded.

"Well, whatever you're calling it, either way, I think some lucky lady will have herself, uh... well let's just say, a rather enjoyable evening."

"So, is that how you see it... she's the lucky one?"

"Well, I mean, what can I say... when you got it, you got it! But you know what... let me just get back to business because if Toni catches me out here flirting with you... she'll ring my neck."

"Oh, come on now... it's not like that, is it?"

"Oh, it's like that! You know she has eyes for you! So anyway, Toni will be showing the property tomorrow at seven pm, while you're enjoying your dinner engagement, or date... or whatever you choose to call it!"

Lee could only smile after ending the call.

Showing The Property

Toni Bradshaw arrived a little early for the showing of the Cross property. She went inside to make sure that everything was in good order. Monica Morgan arrived a little later. Toni went out to greet Monica and the two ladies head back inside.

Once back inside, Toni showed the spacious main level before heading out to the deck. Full of excitement, Monica said, "Wow! Just look at this deck,"

"Isn't it something?" Toni asked.

"It's beautiful!" Monica replied.

"It sure is. Yeah, Mr. Cross is quite an artistic kind of guy. Come... let me show you more, you'll see what I mean."

The two ladies entered the master bedroom.

"And this is the master suite," Toni said.

Monica, very impressed, as she checked out the Arabian style bedroom, said, "Wow... Impressive!"

"I'll say! Kind of makes you wanna climb right on in there, doesn't it?"

"And let your imagination run wild," Monica responded.

Continuing to show the master suite, Toni led Monica into the bathroom, "And a very nice master bath."

"I think I'm falling in love with this place," Monica said. Toni started to make a suggestion, "Well, if you really like it--" Responding very quickly, "I do, I really do," said Monica.

"Great! Then you may wanna think about making an offer because believe me, speaking from experience, I doubt if this property will remain on the market for very long."

They move back through the bedroom on their way out. Monica, still in awe of the bed, "I just can't get over this bed. I should take a picture of it… may I?"

"I guess it'll be okay."
Monica whipped out her cell phone and snapped, not one but, several pictures of the bed and then she went on to snap pictures of the entire room.

Continuing, Toni said, "Also, it may interest you to know that, if you should buy this place, it could all be yours." A bit excited, Monica said, "Really? No, no way! They don't sell bedrooms with homes, do they?"
Toni informed her, "Normally, no. But Mr. Cross has made it very clear, that if a buyer is interested, he would be willing to let all of the furniture and appliances go with the home. He said the less he has to deal with moving, the better."

The lady's finished their tour and head outside. Standing in the driveway, Toni, handed papers to Monica, and said, "So, here is all the information about the property. You'll wanna take some time, look it over, and when you're ready to make an offer, just fill out the forms and get them back to me, and we'll see about getting you into your new home."

CHAPTER

4

Dinner with Michelle And Paula

Seated in a booth at Sterling Steak House, Lee smiled as he received a menu from the server. He started to view the menu. While Lee looked over the menu, Paula arrived. She stood right at the table but did not get Lee's attention upon arrival. Instead, she enjoyed a little humor at his expense as she just stood there watching him as he seemed to be so lost in the menu. After a few seconds, Lee looked up to see Paula, who was just standing there, patiently waiting to see how long it would take for him to notice her.

"Oh, hey," Lee said as he got up to greet her with a warm embrace. "How long have you been standing there?"

"Long enough to see that you were into it pretty deep."

"Now you know you could have said something."

14

"Well, from what I understand, one should not be interrupted when so deep in thought." She whispered to him, "Not to sound too promiscuous or anything but, from what I gather, I believe it's far better to let one finish on their own terms." The subtext was totally understood.

Lee responded, "No argument here!"

Michelle arrived at the restaurant. She entered the foyer where she was greeted by the host. The host took her partway in and pointed to the booth where Lee and Paula were seated. Sitting across from one another, the two seemed to be enjoying each other's company.

Lee was the first to notice Michelle as she was approaching the booth. He got up, "Hey, there she is!"

He also greeted her with a warm embrace, "We were starting to get a little worried about you." While still in his arms, Michelle looked at Paula, "Worried huh?"

Taking his seat, Lee said, "We thought maybe you were gonna cop out on us or something." Looking at Paula, Michelle asked, "And then what?" Paula slid over to let Michelle sit. "Girl… sit down!"

Instead of accepting the space that Paula had made for Her to sit, Michelle opted to take a seat beside Lee. Paula was not exactly happy with Michelle's choice of seating, but she played it off well.

Picking up her menu, Michelle said, "I'm just saying… you guys were not looking so worried if you ask me." Looking at the menu, she continued, "So, let's see now… what looks good on this evening?"

Both ladies believed that the other was interested in Lee for more than just his friendship or a casual dinner. The two ladies looked over the top of their menus and slipped glances at one another with expressions that let the other know, that they were aware of the other's intent, which was to entice Lee.

In a swift and discreet manner, Lee glanced at both ladies as he noticed a little tension between the two. But, wisely so, without comment, he turned his attention back to the menu.

Glancing into her menu, "So, how long have you guys been waiting?" Michelle asked.

"I've been here only about fifteen minutes or so. And Paula just arrived about five minutes before you. But it's all good." Peeping over her menu at Paula, "Well, I guess you two have figured out what you want by now, huh?"

Paula, looking into her own menu, "Uh-huh!"

Michelle then looked at Lee, "And what about you, do you know what you want?"

"Yeah, I believe I do."

"Well, now that we all seem to know what we want, I guess this would be a good time to hear about that, as you put it, 'long story.'"

"Well, it kind of all started after I wrote my first screenplay and submitted it to the Hollywood film festival. Turns out, it got accepted to be in the screening lineup. So naturally, I go to be present at the screenings. I was also fortunate enough to be chosen for an award which included the opportunity to meet, work with, and learn from a few of the well-established professionals in the industry. All the while, my dad was holding on to the idea that I would go to school, become a doctor, and remain right here in Indianapolis."

"Well, that wouldn't have been so bad, now, would it?"

"No, actually it wouldn't, but the heart knows what it wants... and the heart wants... what it wants. And I for one, believe in following your heart. Needless to say, my dad was not happy about my decision to move to California."

"Could he have stopped you?" Paula asked.

"Now, that's a question that has never come up. Actually, I don't think I'd even care to entertain such a thought. Anyway, after my mother passed, I tried talking my dad into moving to California with me, but he wouldn't hear of it. It was only after my sister had a set of twins that she was able to convince him to come and spend some time with his grandkids. And to my surprise, dad came out and liked it, and decided to stay. I'm pretty sure that his

16

decision to stay was largely based on the fact that all four of his remaining siblings live there. Actually, we have more immediate family there, than here.

Now he resides at a very nice senior resort, and he seems to be happy. So, all things considered, we all agreed that it was time to sell the house. And that's about it in a nutshell.

Basically, I just moved to Cali for better accessibility to my craft. Now don't get me wrong… I still love Indy. I was born and raised here. I still have family members here, as well as a few old friends. Indianapolis will always hold a special place in my heart, but the move to Cali was good for my career. I've just recently finished writing my third screenplay, which is currently in production. Life is pretty good right now!"

"Sounds interesting," Michelle said.

Playfully, Paula said, "Yeah, but surely you can find a spot for us, in one of your films. You could write me in as the co-star, and Michelle as a supporting actor."

Michelle responded, "Or… you could write me in as co-star, and Paula… as a supporting actor,"

As they finished their meals, Lee said, "I guess I should thank you ladies, for picking such a great place to dine. This is, without a doubt, the best meal I've had in days."

"Well, you're quite welcome. I'm glad you enjoyed it, Michelle said."

"Yes, absolutely, Paula said, "and if I remember correctly… I believe this place was my idea,"

"Great choice," Lee said, as he looked at Paula.

"Well, you know what they say… the way to a man's heart is through his stomach. So now that you've been well fed, maybe you'll consider staying a little longer," Paula went on to say.

"I'm sure that would be nice, but I really should be getting back to Cali, you know… I'm trying to wrap up this current production."

"Don't you have like… co-producers and directors and stuff like that?"

"Well, Yeah, actually I do. I have a really good

production team out there. But I think it's best, that I'm present on the set, at least as much as possible."

Michelle weighed in, "We understand, business comes first. So, when are you leaving?"

"Tonight actually."

"Will you be needing a ride to the airport?" Paula asked.

"Well, if that's an offer, I really appreciate it, but no... I'm in a rental from the airport. I'll just return the vehicle and be on my way. But as soon as my realtor finds me a buyer, I'll be back to wrap up things here."

"Well, I guess, I... we... will just have to keep an eye on your place till you return," Paula suggested.

CHAPTER
5

Party at The Cross Property

Later into the night, at the Cross property, while Lee was on a plane in route back to California, all the lights were on, and there was loud music playing. Cars packed the driveway and the street. Partygoers were flowing in and out of the house as they were drinking, smoking, and littering.

Paula was home getting ready for bed. She came out of the shower wrapped in a towel. She went into the closet where she put on her pajamas. The TV in her bedroom was on, at a low volume, as it aired a fashion sales program. Paula grabbed a book and sat in the middle of the bed, back against the headboard as she began to read.

Soon, she heard the thumping sounds of car doors shutting. A bit surprised, she looked at the clock, which read 10:49. She hopped out of bed to peep out the window. What she discovered did not sit well with her. She saw a bunch of partygoers getting out of the car and heading toward the Cross property, but only after throwing litter onto her lawn. Quickly, Paula grabbed her cell phone and called Michelle.

Michelle and her daughter Lindsey were sitting in the living room watching a comedy show when the house phone rang. Lindsey got up and walked over to answer the phone, "Hello?"

"Hi Lindsey, this is Paula. I need to speak to your mom!"

"Sure, one moment." Lindsey handed the phone to her mom, "It's Paula, sounds important!"
Michelle took the phone, "Hey girl, what's up?"

"Correct me if I'm wrong, but didn't Lee say that his flight was tonight at 9:15?" Paula asked.

"Yes, I believe that's what he said."

"Then why is it nearly eleven o'clock and there's a party going on at his place?"

"What... A party?" Shocked, Michelle said, "Girl, are you sure?"

"Yes! And I was just about to go to bed, when this carload of hoochie mamas gonna pull up in front of my house, get out, and throw their damn trash in my yard on their way over there! So anyway, I'll fill you in later, cause I'm bout to go check their ass!" Michelle tried to respond, "No-no, wait!" Paula hanged up. Michelle shouted into the phone, "Paula! Paula! Hello!" Michelle hangs up. Lindsey, noticed the worried look on her mom's face, "Mom, what's going on?"

"It seems there's a party going on at Lee's house."

"Yeah... so what's so bad about that?"

"Well, actually, I find that kind of strange, especially since he's supposed to be on a plane right now. He should be about halfway back to California by now. And we were told that the house would remain empty until sold."

Lindsey, realizing what was going down, responded, "P Squad... it's the P Squad, mom!"

"P Squad, what is that?"

"It's a group of thugs that call themselves the Party Squad... P Squad for short. They go around trolling streets and neighborhoods, looking for abandoned houses, homes for sale, empty apartments, even warehouse buildings, and other commercial properties. I heard they will use just about any place that they can get into for a few hours or so, just long enough to throw, what some call, a Drug Fest."

"Oh my God! That's awful!"

"I know, right?"

"How did you find out about all of this?"

"At school you hear a lot about... well, basically everything."

As a concerned parent, Michelle started to ask the question, "Well, you--"
Lindsey heads it off, "No, mom! I would never get involved in something like that. These people are bad, they have guns. I heard that people have gotten shot at some of these events."

Remembering that her best friend, Paula, was on her way over to the Cross property, and could be heading for trouble, Michelle said, "Oh my God! Paula's on her way over there!"

"Call 9 1 1, mom!"

Still in her sleepers, Paula came out of her house and went to pick up the litter, which happened to be an empty four-pack of wine coolers. With the trash in one hand and her cell phone in the other, she stormed her way toward the party. She entered the house and quickly spotted the girl that through the trash onto her lawn. Paula approached the girl from behind. She tapped her on the shoulder. The girl turned around and Paula shelved the empty four-pack of wine coolers into the girl's midsection, "I believe this belongs to you!" The girl and her friends were all shocked, but they didn't dare say anything, as Paula's demeanor was very serious.

Paula moved about, looking around, but found no sign of Lee. She was approached by Watch Boy, one of Frank's thugs who helped to organize this event. "What's up there, mama... in your silk pj's? That's really sexy! So, what can I do for you?"

"Where is Lee?" She asked in a hostile manner.

"I don't know about no Lee, but all you need is me. You know what I'm saying?"

Paula pushed Watch Boy aside and headed over to the stairs where she was met by Randall, who was standing at the bottom of the staircase. He put his arm out, to stop her from going up the stairs. "And just where do you think you're going?"

"I'm going to see Lee... the guy who's over all of this!"

"Well now... that's just a little too bad, because the guy who's over all of this... don't really wanna be bothered. He's kind of busy right now... if you know what I mean!"

Randall looked Paula up and down. He liked what he saw. He continued, "But uh... if you really wanna go upstairs, we can go on up though... if you know what I'm saying!"

Deciding to play her interest card, while slowly stepping around him, "Uh-huh, Yeah, I know what you're saying, and Yeah, I do wanna go on up." She shoved him back, "Just not with you!"

Paula quickly dashed to the top of the stairs only to find Aaron, a bodybuilder, standing guard outside of the door to the master bedroom. He also looked her up and down, "Well now... is this my lucky night or is it yours?" Aaron asked as he flexed his pecks.

Paula realized that the only way she was ever going to find out what was going on inside of that bedroom, and whether or not it had anything to do with Lee, she must first outfox this guy. She decided to play Aaron, by answering his question. "I don't know... you tell me who's the lucky one!"

"Well, what would you like to do baby?" Aaron asked.

Paula, looked Aaron up and down as she slowly walked around him, pretending to be showing interest, by checking him out, when really, she was just positioning herself in front of the door. "Oh, I don't know… depends on what you got… what you working with… know what I'm saying?" Thinking he knew where her mind was, Aaron gets excited, "Oh, I got what you want, and what you need."

By now, Paula had positioned herself between Aaron and the door, as she responded to his comment, "Oh Yeah?" Aaron, who by now had become a bit overly excited, replied, "Hell Yeah!"

Realizing that she has succeeded in getting Aaron to let his guard down, Paula figured now was her chance to get into the room. She shoved Aaron back and burst through the door.

CHAPTER 6

Rape and Murder

In the master suite, Paula found the ringleader, Frank Manning, who was enjoying a make-out session with one of the party girls. Interrupted by Paula's intrusion, he quickly jumped up wearing only his boxers. The party girl, being almost totally exposed, grabbed the sheet to cover herself.

"Yo, what the hell is this?" Franks said to the intruders.

"Hey man, I tried to stop her ass," Aaron said as he tried to respond before getting cut off, "but she just--"

"Nah, it's cool," Frank said as he looked Paula up and down, "So what... you wanna join the party or something? I see you about all dressed for it." The party girl looked a bit displeased at Frank's invite for Paula to join in.

"Where's Lee?" Paula asked in a hostile manner.

Frank took a quick glance at his watch before responding,

"Where is Lee... Damn girl... His ass ought to be about halfway back to California by now."

"So, what the hell are you doing here, and who are you anyway? And how do you know so much about Lee and his business?"

"Well, you see, it's like this... I run this show. It's my business to know things. Though I have never met the guy, hell... I don't even know what the dude looks like, and furthermore, don't give a damn. I just know he won't be back here before I finish my business. Now to answer your question, what am I doing here... well, I was about to enjoy a nice little one on one, that is... until you decided to join in, but it's all good though."

"Actually, it's not all good! And what you need to be doing, is getting your ass, and your little stank ho, the hell out of this house!" The party girl gave Paula a nasty look.

Frank had had enough. He decided to give Paula the low down. "You don't get it, do you? Right here, right now, I'm the boss! And as fine as your ass is, I still don't appreciate you coming in here telling me what the hell I gotta do, bitch!"

Paula slapped Frank's face. He slapped her in return. She fell onto the bed, nearly landing on the party girl. The party girl jumped up and out of the way. Paula jumped up and starts fighting with Frank. Being well conditioned and well trained in self-defense, Paula held her own with Frank until Aaron jumped in, "Damn, this bitch can fight, huh!"

Aaron held Paula's hands behind her back, "Yeah, that's right, hold that bitch still, Frank yelled."
Paula, struggling to free herself, said, "Get off me, let me go you little punk! It takes two of y'all against one woman!"

Frank slapped Paula again, before ripping her top open. Together, the two guys got her subdued on the bed. Frank straddled her. Paula was ranting, "Get your ass off of me, you bastard!" Aaron held her hands while Frank fondled her breasts and taunted her.

"Aw girl… quit playing now… you know you like this. It's what you wanted, ain't it?" He groped her breast. She spat in his face. He grabbed his gun and pointed it in her face, but instead of shooting her, he hit her in the temple with the butt of the gun, knocking her unconscious. Frank began removing her clothes and went on to sexually assault her.

Horrified, by what was taking place right in front of her, the party girl grabbed her clothes and started to leave the room. Paula barely regained consciousness but was very much in a daze. She and the party girl caught one another's eye. The girl's face showed deep concern for Paula, who had been silenced with a cloth in her mouth. Paula's eyes seemed to be asking the girl for help. The girl looked as though she really would like to do something to help, but being so afraid, she opted to save herself by getting out of there as fast as she could.

Paula lost consciousness again. While she was out, the guys had their way with her. Frank, still in his boxers, decided to assault her in oral fashion.

Michelle tried to reach Paula by calling her cell phone. Paula's phone lay on the floor, as it was dropped during the struggle with Frank. Aaron discovered the phone lying on the floor as it began to ring. He picked the phone up from the floor and answered it, "Hello? Hello!" Michelle looked very concerned, as she spoke cautiously into the phone, "May I speak to Paula, please?" Aaron responded, "Oh, is that her name? Well, I'm sorry, looks like Paula's got her mouth full. She can't talk right now." He hanged the phone up and put it in his pocket.

Michelle was concerned about her best friend's safety. She decided, she'd better go and see what's going on.

"They have got Paula, I've gotta go over there!"
Lindsey, who was also frightened, said, "Mom… No! You can't go over there!"

"The police are on the way," Michelle said, "I'll wait until they arrive before going in, but I gotta go over there!"

"I'm coming with you!" Lindsey said.

26

The cops arrived at the Cross property. The partygoers scattered to avoid getting arrested. Randall ran up the stairs to warn Frank and Aaron.

The two guys were having their way with Paula when Randall burst in shouting, "Cops! We gotta get out of here!" Aaron started to gather their belongings.

Again, Paula regained consciousness, though only momentarily, it was long enough to realize what Frank was doing to her. With all her might, she clamped down on his penis with her teeth and ripped it completely off. Frank let out a most horrendous yell as blood spewed out all over the place. Both Aaron and Randall flinched as they could hardly believe what they had just witnessed.

The cops heard the loud yell from Frank. They rushed up the stairs. Aaron pulled Frank a few steps, "Come on man! We gotta get the hell out of here!" Frank stopped, "Wait!" He started back to retrieve his missing body part. Aaron grabbed him again, "Man we gotta go! Come on!"
Frank was enraged. He fired a shot at Paula, striking her in the lower left side of her neck. The bullet traveled upward and exited the right side of the skull, just above the ear.

Topping the stairs, the cops checked every room. They were coming up empty until the sound of gunfire drew them to the master suite. They found Paula, bound to the bed, totally exposed, bloody and unconscious.

Aaron and Randall had helped Frank out to a narrow escape by way of the balcony. The cops noticed the door to the balcony as it was left wide open by the guys trying to make their getaway. Two of the cops rushed over to the balcony and spotted the three guys as they scrambled to avoid capture. After several rounds of gunfire exchanged, Frank and his goons escaped into the night.

Michelle and Lindsey arrived at the Cross property. They got out of their car and approached one of the officers on site. "Hi, I'm Michelle Anderson, chairman of the Homeowners Association here. I need to find Paula."

Inside, in the master suite, cops were present as medics attended to Paula. A female medic discovered what was left of Frank's manhood, in Paula's mouth. She was totally caught off guard as she realized her discovery. She jumped up with a bit of a scream, "Oh my God!" She stepped back to allow the male medic to remove the penis and place it in a plastic container.

Still outside with the officer, Michelle continued, "She's also a member of the H.O.A. She called me about a disturbance. She said that she was coming over here to check it out. Now, she's not answering her phone. I need to know if she's okay."

"Alright, well come with me!" Just as they started to head inside, medics brought Paula out on a stretcher.
Michelle rushed over to try speaking with Paula before they loaded her into the ambulance. She saw the blood all over Paula's face and a big lump about her temple.

"Oh my God, Paula!" Michelle cried.
Paula was still unconscious. Michelle asked the medics, "Is she going to be okay?"

"We're hopeful, ma'am… we're hopeful!" The Male medic said.

The police commissioner approached the chief, "Did we get them?" The chief responded, "No, the sons of bitches got away!" "Got away? What do you mean, got away? All of them?" the commissioner asked. The chief repeated, "They got away!" "The phone lines are on fire. The locals are asking questions, they want answers, The mayor is gonna want answers. What the hell I'm I going to tell him, huh?" The commissioner asked. The chief said, "We were told they were inside. We went in… they ran out. Shots were fired. It's dark. There was a lot of civilians present. Tell the mayor… they got away!!" The commissioner shouted, "This doesn't look good for either of us, you know?" "So, sue me," the chief replied, as he turned and walked away.

Michelle said to her daughter, "come on!"

"Where are we going?" Lindsey asked.

"Home to pack your bags. You're going to Nanna's… I'm going to the hospital!"

Driving in route home, Michelle said to Lindsey, "You may want to pack enough things to get you through for a couple of days. I may be at the hospital for a while."

"Wow! I just cannot believe this has happened to her. I really hope she's gonna be okay," Lindsey said.

"So do I honey… so do I."

Michelle and her daughter arrived back home. In Lindsey's room, Michelle sat on the bed while Lindsey packed her things.

"I know I already said this in the car, but again, be sure to pack everything you'll need for a few days. I'm not leaving the hospital until I know she's stable."

"Okay, but shouldn't someone contact Mr. Cross?"

"Yes, absolutely, someone should."

Michelle took out her cell phone and tried to contact Lee. The phone rang but there was no answer, and his voice mail was full.

Meanwhile, Aaron and Randall had taken Frank to a friend, who happened to be a registered nurse, to receive medical attention under the radar. After attending to Frank, the nurse informed him, of the fact, that over time he should heal just fine. She also told him that after he has had time to heal, he could be fixed up with artificial equipment that will allow pleasure for a partner, but never again for himself.

CHAPTER 7

Michelle At The Hospital With Paula

From the waiting room at the hospital, Michelle tried repeatedly, over the next few hours, to contact Lee. Still, there was no answer. Tired after a long day, Michelle fell asleep. A little while later she woke up and tried calling again.

By now, Lee had made it home and settled in with long time lady friend, Sophia. The two were in bed engaging in a little foreplay. His cell phone rang. At first, he tried to ignore it, but it rang again, and again. Finally, he decided to answer it.

Lee said to Sophia, "Excuse me!" He picked up the phone, "Hello, hello." It was a little too late, Michelle had already hanged up. Turning his attention back to Sophia, "Well, I tried. Now, where were we?" Just as they started to continue their fun, the phone rang again.

"Must be important, maybe you should get it," Sophia said. "Alright, alright," he said as he reached for the phone.

Michelle's persistence had paid off. Lee saw that it was an Indiana number. "Hmmm… an Indiana number, must be about the house." He answered the phone, "Hello? Yeah… what?" He sat up on the side of the bed.

"Oh my God, is she gonna be okay? Yeah, yeah, sure, I'm on my way." After having been home, only for a short period, Lee must now head right back to Indy. He turned to Sophia, "I gotta go! I need you to get me to the airport, ASAP!"

Early in the morning, just before daybreak at North Brook Hospital in Indianapolis, Lee walked into the waiting room and found Michelle asleep in a chair.

Realizing that she must have had a long difficult night, he opted not to wake her, instead, he took a seat beside her where he fell into a deep sleep. He was also exhausted.

Later into the night, a staff member came to Michelle, "I just wanted to let you know that Paula's awake, and you may see her now, but please be advised… she's still in a very fragile state. The blunt force trauma to the head has caused a lot of bruising, as well as clotting in some of the blood vessels in the brain.

We have her on blood thinner medication, hopefully, to prevent any further clotting or a possible stroke. There's also a bullet wound where it made an entry on the left side of her neck and exited the right side of her skull.

Now, as bad as all of this may sound, amazingly so, it did not do a lot of damage. At this point, it's the possibility of blood clots, forming in the brain, that most concern us. She's awake and aware, but much too weak to talk. You can talk to her, only making comments. You should refrain from asking any questions. It would not be good for her to be trying to respond right now."

"Alright, thank you," Michelle said. She was happy to see that Lee had made it in. She woke him and the two went to see Paula in the recovery room. Upon entering the room, they were met by the attending nurse, who offered an additional update on Paula's condition.

"She's had a rough night. She's still very weak and should not try to talk."

"Is she going to be okay?" Michelle asked.

"I'm really not at liberty to offer that kind of a definitive diagnosis. But honestly, all I can say is things are not looking so good right now, and she's aware of that."

The nurse left the room and Michelle moved closer to Paula's bedside. Though Paula was barely conscious, she recognized Michelle and smiled. Paula tried to stretch out her hand, but she could barely move her fingers. Noticing Paula's effort, Michelle took her hand and smiled, "they say you're very weak, and you're not to try talking right now. But I just gotta tell ya... you're one of the strongest people I know. I have to believe that you're gonna be okay!"

Lee stepped up putting his left arm around Michelle's shoulders and with his right hand, he took and held both Michelle and Paula's hands together, "You know, I thought my first words to you would be something like... how are you feeling. But then I thought... boy would that be a dumb question. But I will say this, you are one brave soldier." Paula whispered, "I'm not sure if I'd call it brave or dumb."

"Oh, it was brave. But in light of the outcome, I would much rather you had been a coward that night. You are far more important to us than any old house!" Lee's cell phone rang. He saw that it was the realtor's office calling.

"Excuse me, ladies, I better take this." He stepped away from the bed to talk.

"Hello. Yes, Yeah, sure, okay, alright." He turned back to the ladies, "That was the realtor's office, I'm gonna have to go now. But you take care and try to get some rest. I'll be back to check on you." Both ladies smiled as they nodded their heads okay.

At the realtor's office, Lee sat down with Toni as she explained some of the paperwork. He signed the stack of papers and handed them back to her. After a handshake, Toni escorted him out to the lobby.

Karen sat at her desk, on the phone with a customer. Lee waved bye to her as he passed her desk. She smiled and waved back. Both Karen and Toni watched Lee from behind, with infatuation, as he left heading toward, and disappearing into the elevator.

Later in the evening, while driving along in route to the insurance agency, Lee made a call to Michelle, to see how things were going back at the hospital. Now in her private room, Paula was resting. Michelle's cell phone started to vibrate. She grabbed her phone and answered it.

"Hello?"

"Hey, how's she doing?" Lee asked.

"She's resting."

"Good... good, and how about you, how are you holding up?"

"I'm fine. I'm just glad to see that she's resting comfortably."

"Okay, well just thought I'd check on you. And, uh... just know that I'm by the phone if you need me."

Lee stopped in at the insurance office to discuss the damages to the property, resulting from the unauthorized party thrown by Frank and his gang. "Looks as though your policy is in good standing, and everything should be covered. We'll be getting someone out shortly to make an assessment and then we'll send a crew out to take care of all the damages," The agent said.

Lee shook her hand, "Thank you so much!"

Outside of the insurance office, Lee was about to get into his car. He opened the door, and his cell phone rang. He saw that it was Michelle and took the call while standing outside of the car. "Hey, how's it going?"

Michelle, on the other end of the phone, sitting across the room watching Paula as she sleeps, said, "it's going fine. Paula's still resting and I'm about to head out."

"Good, glad to hear that she's resting. And what about you? You must be starving by now."

"Actually, yes... I am!"

"Well, it'll be my pleasure to take you out for a bite."

"I accept!" Michelle said.

"Alright... same place?" Lee asked.

"Well... how about Vinny's? They have a great breakfast there, that's good any time... day or night!"

"What the lady wants... the lady shall have!"

"Okay. I'll just run-on home, freshen up, and meet you there, say, uh... about an hour or so, give or take a few minutes," Michelle said.

"Works for me!" Lee replied.

A Night to Remember

Lee and Michelle met at Vinny's. The two laughed and talked over a good meal as they enjoyed one another's company. After they had finished, Lee paid the waitress with a fifty-dollar bill. The attractive waitress said, "I'll be right back with your change, sir."

"No-no, keep the change!" Lee said.
She flashed a very warm smile at him, "Thank you very much." He smiled back at her, "You're quite welcome."

"Well, you guys have a wonderful day." Looking straight into his eyes, "And do come back to see us."
He smiled, but with no further comment. The waitress moved on to other customers. Michelle, feeling a bit challenged by the beautiful young waitress, held her peace as they head out to leave.

Once outside, Lee said to Michelle, "Since my place is currently taped off as a crime scene, I was wondering if you could recommend a good hotel?"
"Hotel! Nonsense! I have plenty of room at my place."

"Your place? Are you sure? I mean, I wouldn't wanna be a bother or burden of any kind."

"No, it's fine. It's just me and my daughter, and she's staying with her Nana for a few days."

"Well, alright, if you're sure it's okay."

"It's fine, you can just follow me."

"I'm afraid I'm gonna have to stop for gas, I'm running pretty low."

Michelle took his cell phone, typed in her address, and handed it back to him, "there!" "Okay, I'll just grab some gas and, uh… I'll be right on over."

Michelle got home and slipped into some comfortable silk sleepwear. A little while later, Lee showed up at the door. Michelle answered the door. Lee was a bit smitten with the image he saw before him. He managed to remain cool, calm, and collective, as she invited him in. She gave him a quick tour of her home, including all of the bedrooms, and letting him know that he could settle in wherever he'd like. As inviting and even tempting as everything seemed, like a true gentleman, he chose the guest room.

Michelle commented on the tip that Lee had given the waitress at Vinny's. "So, you're feeling kind of generous tonight, huh?" Lee didn't realize that she was referring to the tip he had given the waitress. He thought that she may be about to suggest something like intimacy between the two of them. He struggled to find a reply. Seeing that he was baffled, Michelle said, "The tip." Still, having not caught on, he looked a bit confused. She continued, "The tip you gave to the waitress." He caught on, "Oh yeah… the tip!"

"Yes… Is that how they do it in Hollywood?"

"Actually, no! That tip would not be considered very generous at all, in Hollywood."

"Well, must be nice. Anyway… should you decide you want a late-night snack or anything, feel free to help yourself." They both look a bit intrigued. Michelle continued, "I guess what I'm saying is, just make yourself right at home."

"Well then, will do!"

Michelle went to her room. Lee settled in the guest room. Later in the night neither he nor Michelle could sleep as they both lay in bed, in separate rooms, thinking of one another. They both contemplated whether or not they should go to the other's room. At about the same moment, after both had become overwhelmed with emotions and curiosities, they found themselves getting up and out of their beds about to head to the other's room.

Lee had made it out into the hallway. Still in her room, Michelle had only made it to her door and was about to grab the knob to open it. They were both stopped in their tracks when they heard the sound of Michelle's cell phone, as it rang. From the hallway, Lee listened as Michelle answered her phone,

"Hello?"

It was the hospital, on the other end, calling to inform Michelle that Paula had taken a turn for the worse. Lee could sense that something was wrong. He headed back to his room. Unaware that Lee had already been up and wide awake, Michelle went to wake him. She politely knocked on the door. Almost immediately the door opened. She realized that the opening of the door was far too immediate for him to wake up, get up, and reach this point without having already been up and alert. Regardless of her conclusion, there he stood, shirtless, in silk boxers.

Michelle enjoyed taking in the view that was before her. She could tell that he was not asleep, but wide awake. Also, she could sense that he was probably going through some of the same emotions that she, herself, had just experienced. After a brief moment of marveling over the view of his masculinity, she quickly set her emotions aside and told him about the phone call she had just received from the hospital. She told him, "I'm gonna have to go to the hospital, and it's pretty late, so you're more than welcome to stay here and try to get some sleep."

"Nonsense, I'll drive you!" Lee said.

At the hospital, the attending nurse tried to make Paula as comfortable as possible. On her way out of the room, she met Lee and Michelle, who were coming in.

"She's been asking for you," The nurse said.

Michelle approached Paula's bedside and took her hand, "As soon as I heard about that group of thugs, girl, I tried to get over there as fast as I could to stop you. I just knew there would be trouble. But don't you worry, those guys are going to pay for what they did to you. So, you just rest and try to get better."

Paula was very weak. She tried to squeeze Michelle's hand. She pulled her a little closer as she tried to speak whispering, "I have a suggestion for the next meeting."

"No, no you should not be trying to talk right now. We can discuss all of that later. You just try to rest."
Paula whispered, "Control the guns!"

"Okay honey, but please, just try to rest now. We'll take care of everything later, I promise. So, please, just take it easy."

Paula, realizing that she was slipping away, uttered her last words to Michelle, "We need better gun control." With her eyes stretched wide, "We need a gun smart nation. Fix it!" She smiled, "I love you!"

After speaking her peace, she closed her eyes for the final time. The monitor flatlined. The attending nurse and other staff members rushed in. They worked with intense efforts to revive Paula, but this time, it was to no avail. They discontinued their efforts.

"I'm very sorry ma'am, we did all we could," the attending nurse said. Michelle turned to Lee. He embraced and consoled her as she sobbed.

A little while later, a staff member came in to get info from Michelle to contact Paula's next of kin. Michelle offered information on Paula's older sister and POA, Sasha Gaines. The staff member left the room and returned moments later, "Okay, I've contacted her sister, Sasha. She'll be coming in for a few days to take care of all the arrangements and the rest of her affairs."

CHAPTER 8

Sasha Comes to Town

After receiving the news of her sister's death, Sasha, a highly successful real estate investor, boarded a flight to Indianapolis on the very next day. In keeping with her DC lifestyle, she hired a private limo, as her means of transportation, while in town. She visited the hospital, where she spoke with the staff and took care of some paperwork. She visited the morgue and identified the body. Sasha was quite poised as she continued with the arrangements.

One week after Paula's death, about midday Saturday, friends and family were gathered at the cemetery. The funeral ceremony had come to a close and people were departing. After paying their last respects, Lee and Michelle head back to their limo. They reached the car and

Lee got the door for Michelle. Before getting in the car, the driver came around to speak to Lee concerning their next destination. Lee pulled out a piece of paper with an address on it. He and the driver stepped away to the front of the vehicle to chat.

In route back to her limo, Sasha, who's being escorted by her driver, stops to greet Michelle. Before Michelle can get into her car, "Michelle," Sasha called out. Surprised that Sasha knows her name, "Yes," Michelle answered.

"Hi, I'm Sasha, Paula's sister. I've heard quite a bit about you."

"Oh really?" Michelle responded.

Sasha went on, "Yeah, whenever Paula would come home, she would always bring pictures of what she called her Indiana family."

"I see!"

Sasha continued, "I recognize you from the picture she refers to as her Indiana big sister."

"We were very close," Michelle said.

"Yes, of course. Well, perhaps I'll see you around," Michelle, not quite sure how to read Sasha, said, "I'm sorry for your loss. You certainly have my condolences."

"Thank you, and likewise," Sasha said.

Michelle offered her business card, "I know you'll be taking care of the rest of her affairs. So, if there's anything I can do please, feel free to give me a call."

Lee was returning to the spot where the two ladies were talking. Sasha got an eye full of Lee as he approached. She responded to Michelle's kind gesture, "Thanks, maybe I will."

Sasha turned to leave before Michelle could make a proper introduction between her and Lee. She knew that she was being watched as she strutted toward her limo. Her appearance was slightly less flamboyant than that of a supermodel on the runway.

Lee, now back at the car, said to Michelle, "Who was that?" "That was Sasha," Michelle responded, "Paula's sister. Not quite sure what to make of her." They got into the limo and left the cemetery.

Monday rolled around and Sasha paid a visit to the A-Team Realty Company. She sat down with the company owner, Toni Bradshaw, as they wrapped up discussions concerning the sale of her sister's home.

"Okay, well… it looks like I have everything I need here to set things in motion. So, I will get right on it. And as always, we hope for a speedy sale," Toni said.

Getting up to leave, Sasha said, "Yes, let's hope so!"

Toni walked her to the door and with a handshake, "I wanna thank you for your business, and we'll be in touch."

Leaving Toni's office, on her way out, Sasha strutted through the lobby. As she passed Karen's desk, "Have a nice day," Karen said. Without breaking a stride, Sasha responded only with a fake smile that seemed to suggest something like, you're beneath me and I don't care to speak to you. At least, that's what Karen got from Sasha's response. Needless to say, Karen was offended.

She returned a snobby gesture right back to Sasha, but she didn't notice, as she headed on out.

Later in the day, at the Cross property, Lee was outside removing some police tape when Sasha's car rolled by. Sasha saw Lee and told the driver to stop. Lee took notice as the limo came to an abrupt stop and began to back up. The rear window on the driver's side went down. Lee recognized Sasha as he approached the car.

"I hope I'm not disturbing you," Sasha said, "but I couldn't help but notice you're removing the tape. I know this is the place where my sister was attacked. I was just wondering if I may—"

Realizing what she wanted to ask, "Would you like to come in?" Lee asked.

"May I?"

"Sure!"

Lee got the car door and escorted Sasha into the house. They entered the master bedroom. Sasha walked over to the bed. She took a deep breath. "So, this is it… the spot where my sister met her demise. I've heard some of the details. I know she put up a good fight.

She's always been a fighter." Sasha weakened and turned to Lee for comfort. Like a true gentleman, he consoled her.

A representative from the real estate office came to take pictures of the property. Unknowingly, she captured images of Lee and Sasha through a second-floor window as they were locked in an embrace.

Just as the real estate rep was capturing the final images, the front door opened and there was Lee, exiting the home, with Sasha on his arm as he escorted her back to her car.

The next morning at A-TEAM REALTY, Karen sat at her desk going through some mail. She discovered an envelope with pictures taken of the Cross property. Inside of the envelope was plenty of good images, however, there were a couple of shocking images that were sure to be displeasing to the boss. In the background of one of the pictures, Karen recognized Lee and Sasha in the window. In the second picture, she noticed the two coming out of the house, arm in arm. Of course, her mind would jump to conclusions. Karen said to herself, "Okay… Toni's gonna wanna see this." She took the pictures to her boss.

Toni sat behind her desk doing some paperwork. Karen walked in and Toni addressed her upon entry, but without looking up, "Yes, Karen?"
Karen approached Toni's desk saying, "Thought you might want to take a look at these pictures before they go into print." Toni looked up. Karen handed over the envelope.

"Pictures of what?" Toni asked.

"Pictures of the Cross property," Karen said.

"Oh great!" As she thumbed through a few images, "We can get them into the next run."

"Well, you might wanna take a closer look at the images in the background of the last two," Karen said, "before you decide on that."

Toni took a closer look and being not a fan of Sasha, was very displeased by what she saw.

"Get Marissa in here, now!" Toni yelled. Karen turned to head out to get Marissa, but just as she opened the door,

Marissa was standing right there as she was just about to knock.

"Just the person I was coming to get," Karen said. She makes a head nodding gesture toward the boss's desk, "Front and center girly!"

Marissa walked in. Toni rose out of her seat holding the pictures up toward Marissa, "What the hell is this? Did you not notice the images in the background?"

Marissa tried to respond, "Yes, but I--" She was cut off by Toni.

"Just be glad we caught it before it went into print."

"Yeah, well, uh… about that… it kind of already did."

"What are you talking about… how can that be?" Toni said, "I have the prints right here."

"Actually, those are copies. For whatever reason… when I went to pick up the pictures there were double copies in the envelope. So, I thought I'd speed things along by delivering one set to the editor last night," Marissa said.

"Even without approval… why would you do that?"

"I did question whether we should run them, but he told me not to worry about it. He said that he would add a caption and put a spin on it in such a way that, it would likely speed up the sale."

Toni took her seat, "I mean… we're trying to sell a home here…. not some kind of penthouse or… well, whatever!" She sighed and took a moment to collect herself.

"Well, I guess, what's done is done. So, he's gonna put a spin on it, huh… for a quicker sale. Well, I can hardly wait to see the paper!"

Later in the evening, Michelle arrived home. She pulled into her driveway, got out of her car, and went to the mailbox. She collected her mail and the newspaper before going inside. In the living room, Michelle sat on the sofa as she went through the mail. After checking the mail, she started looking through the newspaper. Soon, she came to the real estate section. She could hardly believe her eyes, but BAM, there it was, plastered across the front page, the Cross property, with images of Lee and Sasha standing near the window, as they were locked in an embrace. The caption reads, "This loving home awaits the perfect loving couple." With a solemn stare at the images, Michelle wondered what exactly was going on between Lee and Sasha.

CHAPTER 9

2nd Neighborhood Meeting

On the next evening, following the discovery of images of Lee and Sasha in the paper, Michelle spoke at another neighborhood meeting. "I'm sure, by now, most of you have heard about the tragic event that occurred just down the block from where we are right now." An H.O.A. member responded, "Yeah, I never thought I'd see anything like that take place around here." A second H.O.A. member said, "Me neither, I mean, I thought maybe a break in or robbery or something, but never anything like that." A third member added, "It's time to get tough with these criminals. I know that, throughout the city and around the country, there has been a lot of neighborhood meetings, city council meetings, congressional meetings, meetings for crime watch and prevention programs, but... the end result is always the same.

Never enough gets done to really make a difference. I say… it's time to get tough on these criminals, and I mean, really tough!"

"You're absolutely right," Michelle said, "I couldn't agree with you more. But the question is… how do we go about doing that? How do we make our voices heard, and to whom it will really make a difference?"

Sasha, who had been sitting near the back of the room, got up and head toward the front. Michelle was surprised as she was not even aware that Sasha was present. Sasha, spoke along the way to the front, "I'm so glad you asked. I believe I can help." She reached the front and flashed a quick smile to Michelle, before turning to address the crowd.

"Hello everyone. My name is Sasha Gains. Though I reside in Washington, D.C., I can assure you that no one here is more bothered by the tragedy that took place down the way, than I am! Paula was my little sister."

Michelle, who had remained standing, now took her seat. Sasha continued, "And yes sir! I agree as well… it's time to get tough. I want to see all of these criminals caught and brought to justice." The crowd agreed, their voices shouted, "Yeah, that's right!" Sasha continued, "Mr. Cross was nice enough to show me the bedroom where my sister was attacked."

There was much curiosity stamped across Michelle's face. Sasha continued, "After several days of police investigations, imagine my surprise to find, still lying on the bed, my sister's pendant." She held the pendant up to the crowd. She then held up the one she was wearing, "Just like the one I'm wearing right now."

Sasha began to get a little emotional. The crowd seemed to share her pain. She continued, "When we were kids, still in grade school, our mother gave each of us one. She said to us, 'As you grow, life can sometimes, take you in different directions. But as long as you have these, you'll always have something to help you, to not only remember me, but also, to remember one another.'"

Sasha took a moment to settle herself before continuing. "My home is Washington, D.C. My sister's home was here in Indianapolis, the place she loved… with all of you… the people she loved. I can recall many times, her referring to Michelle as her Indiana big sister." Michelle wore a soft smile. Sasha turned to Michelle, and handed the pendant to her, "I'm certain she would want you to have this. Guess this makes you my Indiana sister now."

Sasha turned back to the crowd, "So anyway, I've heard a little bit about the 'MOVEMENT,' if you will, that some of you have thought about trying to initiate. Well, it just so happens, that uh… politically speaking, I'm pretty well connected there in DC. So yeah… when it comes to something as important as better gun control, I believe that I can be a great deal of help, at least as far as, getting the ball rolling."

The crowd seemed quite pleased to hear that they now have a voice in Washington. Sasha went on to say, "Lee and I… Mr. Cross, that is… had a rather lengthy conversation concerning this whole ordeal." Again, there was the look of curiosity and distrust stamped across Michelle's face. Sasha said, "This tragedy happened to my sister, and it happened in his house. That in itself… kind of creates a bit of a bond between us." Michelle certainly did not care to hear that statement, but being the professional that she was, one would never notice as she kept her cool, as Sasha continued, "So, we've both decided to stick around for a while and join you in this fight for greater gun control." About the last thing Michelle would have wanted to hear, was that Sasha would be sticking around for a while.

On the next evening, Lee and Michelle sat in a booth opposite one another at a popular steakhouse restaurant.

"I missed you at the meeting last night, was kind of hoping to see you there," Michelle said.

"And there I would have been, had I not been in a meeting with my real estate agent.

It turns out the activity on the house has gone cold."

"What does that mean?"

"Well, according to Toni… she was pretty sure she had a buyer, that was until the news got out about the incident that happened at the house."

"Sorry to hear that."

"But it's okay."

"So, what now?"

"Well, Toni said I should just be patient and not to worry. She said… she's seen this kind of thing before. It will all blow over soon and sales activity should return to normal."

"Guess this means you'll be staying awhile, huh?"

"Yeah, kind of… well actually… I think it means that I'll probably be back and forth quite a bit."

"I see! So, have you been staying at the house?"
Responding rather slowly, "No, but, as of tonight, I'll be back in there." He was starting to pick up on her line of questioning. It became obvious what she must be thinking.

"So where have you been staying?"
Still a little slow to respond, "The Royale," Lee answered.

"The Royale," Michelle responded, "wow! Good choice! A mighty fancy place to be spending nights alone."

"Well, what can I say… that's how it's been. And I really wanna thank you for opening your door to me, before. But you know, with your daughter returning home and all… uh… well, it just didn't seem like a good idea for me to be hanging around, or especially to be spending the night there, you know?"

"Uh huh. So anyway… Sasha mentioned that you guys have been spending time together…" Michelle took a brief pause, as she looked for some kind of reaction, but coming up empty, she continued, "…talking about our crime situation, and that both of you have decided to stay and help."

"Yes, that's right!"
Michelle looked firmly into his eyes as she tried to read more into this Sasha situation than what was being said.

47

"Well, that's nice," she said, "I think I can speak for the entire committee, in saying, we're happy to have you guys aboard. We'll take all the help we can get. I heard you had some really great ideas, can't wait to hear them. But what about Hollywood?"

"Well, between Hollywood, Indianapolis and DC, I guess I'll be collecting quite a few frequent flyer miles."

"DC? Why DC?" Michelle asked.

"Well, without saying who, what, when, or where, but somewhere out west, a group came together and conducted a few serious crime prevention operations, that worked out really well, using what we call The Gunsmart System. I may have shared some of that information with Sasha."

"The Gunsmart System... Hmm... Sounds interesting." Still on her personal fishing expedition, "So, did you guys discuss all of this at The Hotel Royale, or out to dinner someplace as we are now?"

"No, actually, it was during her very brief visit to the crime scene. Anyway, turns out... she would like me to meet with some of DC's authoritative figures, who she believes can add a lot of legal and political weight to what we would be trying to accomplish." Michelle was not quite sure just how she felt about all of this.

Trip to Washington

A few weeks after Paula's death, Sasha had returned home to Washington, to set up meetings and make plans for Lee's visit. Early Monday morning, of the following week a plane descended over DC. Lee, accompanied by Michelle, made his way through the airport and into a limo that had been arranged for him, by Sasha.

The couple arrived at the capitol building. An elevator opened on the second floor, and out came Lee and Michelle. They stopped at the reception desk to sign in. The receptionist escorted them to the room where Sasha and her friend, Congressman Walthall Hendricks (Walt), awaited as they were caught up in a moment of embracing.

The receptionist got the door. Sasha and Walt responded quickly by putting some distance between themselves. Sasha turned to greet Lee and Michelle as they entered the room. Checking her watch, cheerfully, Sasha said, "Well, right on time... prompt, I like that." She spoke to Michelle, "Michelle, my Indiana sister... wasn't really expecting you..." She played everything off well, by giving Michelle a warm embrace, as though she was really happy to see her, "...But it's great to see you... so glad you came!"

If there is one thing Michelle is not, it's naive. She wasn't fooled for one minute. She was very much aware of the fact that Sasha would like nothing more than to sink her claws into Lee.

Sasha introduced everyone. "Lee and Michelle... I'd like you to meet my good friend, Congressman Walthall Hendricks. And Walthall... this is Mr. Leander Cross and Michelle Anderson." They greeted one another properly with a handshake. Lee addressed Walthall, "So nice to meet you, sir... call me Lee!"

"Feeling's mutual... everyone calls me Walt!"
Michelle extended her hand to Walt, "Pleasure to meet you, sir." He responded while taking her hand, "Walt!"
Michelle responded, "Walt! Yes... it's a pleasure!"

Still holding Michelle's hand with both of his, Walt said, "Well Sasha's given me a bit of a briefing on what it is you're trying to do, and believe me, the pleasure's all mine. I couldn't agree more, we really need to do something. Gun violence in America is certainly on the rise. It has become a commonplace in our nation. And I am certainly in favor of anything that will bring this situation under control."

Sasha invited everyone to sit. "Come, please... sit." They all took their seats as Lee reveal only a little bit of information about his pitch for tomorrow's big meeting with some of DC's power players.

CHAPTER 10

A Night in D.C.

Later in the evening, Sasha, Lee, and Michelle arrived at one of Sasha's favorite restaurants. Not expecting Lee to be accompanied by Michelle, Sasha had called the restaurant a few days earlier and had already prearranged to have a table reserved for two, Lee and herself. Upon arrival, Sasha gave her name to the host, "Gains." The host looked at the list, "Yes, I have here Gains, table for two." Sasha was quick to respond, "Three!" The host looked back at the list again. "Hmmm!... Someone wrote table for two. Okay, well uh… no problem, just give me a minute, I'll be right with you." The host went to have a table prepared for three. Michelle, taking it all in, knew exactly the kind of evening Sasha had originally planned. She and Sasha exchanged smiles as they waited patiently for the host to return. The host returned and showed them to their table.

The three sat in a booth enjoying dinner and sipping fine wine. Michelle sat beside Lee and Sasha was seated across the table. Sasha said, "Well, I thought today's meeting went pretty well."

"Yes, it did," Michelle said.

"Yeah, and as far as the big meeting tomorrow, we have a very large number of signed petitions that we plan to present," Lee commented.

"From what I've seen in politics, signed petitions are always a plus," Sasha replied.

"Yeah, and we're hoping that it will add quite a bit of weight to the overall presentation, you know?"

"I'm sure it will all go well. I have faith in you. Somehow, I sense that you're the kind of guy who can get just about whatever he wants." Sasha's comment, to Lee, rubbed Michelle the wrong way. She gave Sasha a quick glance of disgust. Sasha continued, "And if your presentation helps lead to the capture of all the guys, involved in my sister's murder, and others like them... I'm all in."

Time passed as the three shared a few ideas about gun control. They finished their meals and made their exit. Sasha's limo pulled up in front of the restaurant. They loaded in and off they went. By Sasha's request, the driver took them on a bit of a tour, showing them some of DC's popular sights and points of interest.

After a tour of the town, they pulled up to a beautiful mansion.

"Why are we stopping here?" Michelle asked.

"This is our final destination for the night. This is where I live. This is home!"

It now became quite clear that Sasha, an avid investor, has done very well for herself especially in the real estate arena. Sasha invited them in. She got the door, "Please, come in... and welcome to my humble abode."

"Girl stop... this is anything but humble," Michelle said.

Looking around, Michelle continued, "You have a lovely home."

"Well, thank you."

"Just you here?" Michelle asked.

"Just me!"

"What in the world do you do with such a large place?"

"Well, you know, if you make it, you have to invest it, or they take it, right?"

"You got a point there!"

"Besides, I entertain quite a bit. Come on, let me show you around."

Sasha gave Lee and Michelle a tour of the mansion. First, she took them to the upper level and showed a TV room and several nice bedrooms including a couple with fireplaces. Returning to the main level, she showed an office, a study, a huge family room, a formal dining room as well as a second dining room. On the lower level, she showed a huge game room and a theater. Outside, she showed the pool, a Jacuzzi, and a Cabana.

Rounding off the tour of her home, back inside, she came down a hallway to show them a couple of guest rooms on the main level. Sasha said to Michelle, "here's a room I thought you might like. It has soft colors, kind of ladylike, you know?"

"Very nice... thank you!"

She led them down the hall to the next room, which was closer to hers.

To Lea she said, "and here's one with darker colors. More manly, don't you think?"

"Yeah, great, I'll take it!"

On to the next room, which was her master suite, Sasha said, "And this is the master suite." Completely blown away by the view of the master suite, Michelle said, "Wow! It's really beautiful. And I thought the room upstairs with the gorgeous fireplace was the master."

"Technically... this is!"

"So, which one do you sleep in?" Michelle asked.

"Uh… it just depends."

"On?"

"Whatever I'm feeling at the moment."

Michelle, still very much aware of Sasha's original intent, "I see!"

Continuing the tour, Sasha showed them where to get anything that they would need or want. "There's linen here, a bath there, as well as at the other end of the hallway. And, the kitchen is right this way, just beyond my room and another bath. So, just make yourselves right at home. There's fruit, snacks, water, wine, and if you would like something a little stronger, just look in the cabinet to the right of the fridge."

"Thanks for the tour," Lee said, "you have a lovely home! I think I'll just go look over my notes a bit and try to prepare for our meeting tomorrow. Good night ladies."

"Good night," Michelle said.

"Good night, sleep well," Sasha said.

Off to his room, Lee went. The ladies bid one another good night and were off to their rooms.

Later in the night, Lee got up to go to the bathroom. Sasha was awake. She knew that it was Lee, who had gone into the bathroom. She got up and headed to the kitchen, wearing her nighties. Lee stepped out of the bathroom, into the hallway, to head back to his room. Sasha, standing in the doorway of the kitchen, got his attention. "Ahem!"

Lee turned around and was totally shocked to see Sasha standing there in her fancy sleep apparel.

"Oh, you startled me a bit. I wasn't expecting to see anyone standing there."

"So, are you disappointed?"

"Well, no… I'm not saying that!"

"I was just about to have a little hot toddy to help me sleep, join me!" Lee stepped to the doorway of the kitchen, "Well uh… I better not."

"Why not?" Sasha asked.

"Well, it's--"

Sasha cut in, "Is it Michelle… are you two--"

"Oh, no-no… nothing like that," he responded.

"Well, what then?" she asked.

"Well, you know… it's just… I don't know… it just doesn't seem quite proper. I mean… we're all just kind of getting to know one another, you know?" Sasha stepped very close upon him, "Well, what better way to get to know one another."

"You're not making this very easy on me, you know? Actually… you're making it kind of hard." Standing really close, Sasha looked up into his eyes, "I'm making it hard?" She looked down at his crotch and back up into his eyes, "So I am! This speaks volume, don't you think?" Taking another look she continued, "Lots, and lots, of volume!"

Michelle, lying in bed, was awakened by the mumbling sounds of Lee and Sasha's voices. Throwing back the covers, a book that she had been reading before falling asleep, flew off of the bed, making a loud smashing sound as it hit the floor.

Lee and Sasha heard the noise that Michelle made as she was getting out of bed. They quickly put some space between themselves as Sasha closed and tied her nightgown. They suspected that Michelle's next move would be coming to check things out. Their suspicions were spot-on. Michelle's door opened, and down the hall, she came to the kitchen. She approached the two of them, "What's going on here?"

"We were just about to have a little nightcap. Join us!" Sasha said.

"No, thank you!" Michelle said, "I think what we all need is to just get some sleep! We have a very important engagement tomorrow!" Lee responded, "And I think you're right. We need to focus on our goal. Goodnight ladies." Lee head to his room and shut the door. Once again, the two ladies were left alone to bid one another Goodnight.

CHAPTER

11

Big Meeting on The Hill

(First Pitch)

On the second day of Lee's visit to Washington, he sat in a board room of the capitol building, along with Michelle and Sasha, among some of DC's top officials. Lee finished his pitch, "So, that's pretty much it, what has been tested and proven to work well, what we're trying to accomplish and how we might go about it." The content of his pitch caught everyone by surprise.

Congressman, Jack Wilson, looked at Walt, then at another congressman, then back to Walt. Walt looked at Sasha. Lee, taking it all in, knew what they were thinking. He responded, "Don't blame her, she didn't know. I did not disclose the full details of this idea to her. I did not want to risk scaring you guys away before having a chance to meet with you."

Congressman Wilson said to Walt, "May I speak to you for a moment, please... in private?" The two men got up out of their seat to excuse themselves, but before they could leave the room, Lee continued, "Look guys, I understand full well what I'm asking, but I also understand just as well... the kind of results that can be achieved from such measures. It's been tested several different times, in several different areas. The result is always the same, a win-win situation." The two congressmen did not leave the room, instead, they returned to their seats.

Now, with everyone's undivided attention, Lee continued, "So, why am I here? Well, all of the tests that I've just spoken about were conducted without any kind of legal authority. And yet, in every case, they yielded very good results. In the areas tested, we saw crime reductions of over ninety-five percent. I don't know of any other crime prevention program, that has ever yielded those kinds of results. Now, you add legal authority, coupled with proper law enforcement to the equation... and it'll just make this idea a whole lot bigger, and a whole lot better. I believe it'll be the best thing we've seen in over a century.

As of right now, when it comes to the safety of the American citizens, we have a broken system... a very... broken system. This idea, that I propose to you, will fix a very large part of that system. I don't know about the whole make America great again idea, but this idea... will certainly make America safe... again!

Just a few weeks ago I witnessed a dying woman utter her last words on her death bed saying, and I quote, 'We need to make America a gun smart nation.' The idea that I present to you will do just that. Now, who in here would dare tell me that this idea doesn't, at least warrant some serious consideration."

Everyone in the room started to eyeball one another.
Congressman Wilson spoke out, "Listen, I understand your passion, and your desire to fix a very bad problem.

You wanna make the whole world a better place. And you say… that you understand what you're asking. Well, I'm not so sure that you do." All eyes were on Lee. He held his peace. Wilson started to speak with more intensity, as he continued, "This thing you're asking would actually challenge the constitution of the United States of America. Need I remind you, sir, that these are the core values by which this nation stands!"

Lee, now getting intense in his own right, "And when was the constitution written?"

"What? What the hell does that have to do with anything?" Wilson shouted.

"Just tell us, when was it written, sir?" Lee asked.

"1787, and to this day, it's still one of the greatest set of articles this nation has ever recorded, sir!"

"Oh yeah? So, tell us… how many drive-bys do you think they had at that time, sir? How many carjacking's do you think they had? How many home invasions? Do you think they had social media back then… influencing our young to commit all kinds of hate crime… bullying some to the point of suicide? How about armed robberies and homicides, huh? Surely there must have been a whole bunch of school shooting's going on waaaay back in the seventeen hundred's… sir!"

"Alright, alright… we get the picture," Congressman Wilson responded.

"Do you?" Lee asked.

Wilson continued, "Times have changed. So, what are you saying?"

"What I am saying, is that perhaps it's time the constitution undergo a little revision." At that comment, you could have heard a pin drop. It was as if he had just said something outrageous and very offensive.

Finally, Congress Woman Leanne Litchfield responded, "Sir, the people will never go for that."

"On the contrary, many already have," Lee said.

"Yes, I'm aware that you have a few names, but I can assure you that's barely a drop in the bucket, as opposed to the entire nation," Litchfield said.

"Even if we agreed with you, who in this room of sound mind would be courageous enough to present such an idea to the house?" Wilson asked.

"Given the opportunity... I would," Lee replied.

"Well, that'll never happen. No one outside of the house can present a bill." There was a moment of silence. Walt, shocking all of his constituents, "I'll do it." Another moment of brief silence, this one accompanied by the stares of astonishment. Wilson said to Walt, "You're kidding, right?"

"No!... No, I'm not!"

Wilson, forcefully closing his notebook, "Well, good luck to the both of you... you're gonna need it!"

About midday, on the next day, outside of Sasha's home, a limo waited to take Lee and Michelle back to the airport. The three, Sasha, Lee, and Michelle, all stood near the car as they said their goodbyes.

"Well, I really enjoyed having you guys. I wish you could stay longer," Sasha said.

"It's been a pleasure," Lee responded.

"Yes, and I really hope that we've accomplished something," Michelle added.

"Oh, I wouldn't worry at all," Sasha said, "you've handed the ball off to Walt, now. If there's anybody who can get it to the goal line, it's him."

"Great! Well, guess we better be going." Lee gave Sasha a hug and then stood back by the rear door of the car, while Michelle and Sasha hugged and said their final goodbyes.

"Hopefully, I'll see you back in Indy, pretty soon. Just waiting to hear from the realtor."

"Okay, well, you have my number, call me. My door is always open to you," Michelle said.

"I will, thanks."

Lea and Michelle got into the car. They all waved, bye, as the car pulled away.

Riding along, in route to the airport, "That was nice of you," Lee said to Michelle.

"What was?" Michelle asked.

"Extending your hospitality for Sasha to come and stay with you."

"Well, I mean, she just put us up for a while, in a very nice mansion. So, what am I to do, reject her if she should come to my little spot? After all, she is my DC sister now, right?" He looked at her with a slick grin.

"What?" she asked.

Still grinning, "Nothing," he said.

"Okay, nothing!... You may as well say it… it's all over your face."

"Well, you seem to be somewhat distrusting of her."

"Somewhat distrusting, huh… Should I be? I mean, can you think of any reason why I should be somewhat distrusting of her?" Lee raised both hands in surrender fashion, "Hey, you know what, I've probably already said too much. I am not gonna touch that. But anyway, on a more serious note, hopefully, Walt can, as your DC sister put it, 'Get the ball to the goal line.'"

"Yes, hopefully."

"Either way, if you hear from them first, you call me. If I should hear from them first, I'll call you. We can then, set up a meeting with the local authorities, to get the ball rolling toward making Indianapolis a safer place to live."

Michelle responded, "I can hardly wait!"

Arriving at the airport, "You know, this part feels a little strange," Michelle said.

"What do you mean?" Lee asked.

"Well, we came out here on the same flight, and now, we're leaving on separate flights. But I understand… different destinations… different directions."

"Actually, it's the same direction," Lee said, "It's just that your destination is a whole lot closer than mine." Though she never let on to it, Michelle couldn't help but wonder if Lee would be taking a flight at all, since her flight was originally scheduled to depart a few minutes prior to his.

As it turned out the flight to Indianapolis was delayed by about thirty minutes, thus causing Lee to be the first to depart. While awaiting her flight back to Indianapolis, Michelle was quite pleased, and relieved, to watch Lee board his flight back to California.

CHAPTER

12

Hearing From Washington

A few days had passed since Michelle's visit to Washington. The house phone in the living room began to ring. There was no one present in the room. Lindsey sat on a stool at the bar in the kitchen, reading a book. She could hear the phone as it rang, but chose to ignore it, assuming that her mom would soon answer it.

Michelle was in the laundry room. The noise of the washer and dryer drowned out the ringing of the phone. Lindsey, realizing that her mom must have been preoccupied, went to answer the phone, "Hello, yes, one moment please." She went and found her mom doing laundry. Handing the phone to her mom, "You have a call from Washington. Sounds important!"

Michelle took the phone, "Hello, oh yes, Walt. So glad to hear from you." Lindsey headed back to the living room. On the phone, Michelle continued, "I really hope you have some good news for us."

"I have news," Walt said.

"Okay, so, should I sit? Do I need to brace myself or--" Walt cut in, "Well, after meeting with some of the other congressmen out here, a few of us thought it might serve you well to employ a tactic such as, or much like that of a blue law."

"A blue law? Okay...?"

"Have you heard of such?" Walt asked.

"Yeah, I've heard of such, but I can't say that I'm well versed on it, I mean as far as how to go about initiating such a thing, or its guidelines or limitations."

"Well, don't sweat it. As it happens, congressman Andrew Carrington was present at the meeting. He was intrigued by you guys' idea. He plans to be in Indianapolis in a couple of weeks, and he's agreed to meet with you guys to help guide you through the process of getting the ball rolling."

"That certainly sounds like good news to me."

"As I said before, it's news. Perhaps you've heard the phrase 'there are no guarantees in life,' well, that's times ten when it comes to politics."

"Yeah, but as long as it's a legal strategy, and it saves lives I think it'll be well worth a try." Still on the phone, Michelle walked back into the living room where her daughter sat reading her book. Her phone conversation came to a close, "Okay, thank you for calling and for all your help." Walt responded, "you're quite welcome and do keep in touch." "Alright, I sure will, bye-bye now." She replaced the receiver on the base.

"Is everything okay?" Lindsey asked.

"Yeah... it's just that this whole, crime control, gun control, thing seems likely to become quite a challenge."

"Well, I think that whatever you can do, to put even a dent in some of these crimes, no matter how big or small, if it prevents at least one murder, just one innocent life saved, then I say it's well worth the challenge," Lindsey said. Michelle responded, "You're so right, dear... You are so right!"

Back in Hollywood, Lee was on the set, directing his latest movie project. His cell phone vibrated. He saw that it was Michelle calling. He motioned to Tyler, his co-producer, that he was taking a call. He moved to a quiet location to talk, "Hey, Michelle, how are you?"

"I'm fine, and how are you?"

"Great, actually things are going very well. We're just here on the set, doing what we do, trying to wrap up our latest project."

"Oh, I'm sorry, I hope I didn't catch you at a bad time."

"No, it's fine. Tyler can handle the set. So, what's up?"

"Well, I heard from Walt today."

"Well now... and how did I know that you would be the one he would choose to contact."

"Oh, stop... don't even go there!"

Lee chuckled, "Anyway... good news I hope!"

"As it turns out, for the most part, they felt that we could be on to something."

"Good deal. I knew that some of them would see things our way."

"But, as it stands, no one's really willing to suggest imposing a federal mandate that would challenge any part of the United States Constitution," Michelle added.

"So, what are you saying... they all punked out?"

"No-no... now, let's not jump to conclusions. Actually, what he did was offer up some pretty good advice."

"Advice huh. Okay, so, what have they got for us?"

"Walt says that actually, this is not the first time that he's heard of an idea similar to this. But it is the first time since he's been in office, that anyone's ever tried to move on it."

"Oh really?"

"Yeah, and his suggestion for us would be to try to go local with the idea first."

"Go local, huh? Well, you know I already--, well fine, what else?"

"Well, he's already spoken, to our State Congressman Andrew Carrington, about the matter."

"Great! So, is he on board?"

"Well, he'll be here in a couple of weeks. I don't think that he'll be planning on leading the march on the whole deal. But I'm told that he'll be willing to guide us through the process of creating and presenting a bill for possible consideration."

"Alright then... sounds like a plan. Guess I'll be seeing you in a couple of weeks."

"Okay, great. I shall look forward to it."

"Me too. Take care now," Lee said.

CHAPTER

13

INTERROGATION ROOM

Seven weeks had gone by since Paula was murdered. Police were still conducting investigations into the events that led to her death. Early Monday morning, Sargent Lucas Perkins sat at a table in the interrogation room across from Natasha Wells. She had been present and apprehended at the Cross property on the night of the tragedy that ultimately claimed the life of Paula Gaines. Natasha was only one of many who had been brought in for questioning and was also the one that Sargent Perkins believed to be the most credible.

"Now listen Natasha, right now you need only to think about yourself and your little girl… Okay? Now, we just need the names of the guys who arranged this party," Perkins said. Natasha, tired of being asked the same questions, several different times, by several different officers, said, "Man, I don't know their names. I already told your detectives, the first time they dragged me down here, I don't know them. And I'm getting sick and tired of your people dragging me down here week after week asking me the same old questions. My story's not gonna change. I'm telling you the truth... I don't know these guys, okay?"

"Well," Perkins said with a very stern look at Natasha, "here's the thing... you were busted at a party that was put on by these guys. And yet, you say you know none... of them?"

"None!" Natasha responded.

"So, what were you doing there? Did someone invite you, or did you just take it upon yourself to be there trespassing?" Perkins asked.

"Yes... I was invited! And no... I was not trespassing!"

"Actually, you were... you all were. See, here's the thing... the fact that the owner knew nothing about this event, and therefore, invited no one on to his property, kind of put's you all in the category of trespassing."

"Wow! I just wish I'd stayed home that night,"

"I'm sure you do," Perkins said. He continued, saying,

"Well, I gotta tell you, should the owner decide to press charges, when tied to a murder, trespassing can be a very serious offense, with sentencing as high as ten years behind bars."

"And for what... just one dumb night of partying,"

"Well, don't beat yourself up too bad about it just yet," Perkins said, "I'd like to help you if I can. But first, you gotta help me, so I can help you... Okay? So, let's back it up a bit. Now, how did you first hear about this party?"

"I first heard about it earlier that same day when Serena invited me."

"And what is your relationship with Serena?"

"She's been my friend and co-worker for the past four years."

"Did she mention that this would be a squatters party?"

"No!"

"Have you ever heard of, or ever attended a squatters party before?"

"No! Absolutely not… at least not that I'm aware of! I mean… well Yeah, I've heard of them… but I've never been to one, that is, before now. And I would have never gone to this one, had I known what it was."

"Well, did your friend Serena clue you in once you got there?"

"No."

"No? So… your friend just decided to keep that bit of information from you, is that it?"

"I never saw her that night. She never showed up."

"She never showed up? Now let me get this straight… your friend invites you to a squatter's party, she never shows up, and you get busted for trespassing. Wow!... Well, that kind of sucks, now, doesn't it?"

"Yeah, it does. But like myself, Serena's a single mom, back at home with her parents. We don't get out much. So, it seemed like a good opportunity to get out and just have a little fun and unwind a bit, you know?"

"Yeah, I get that… but what happened to your friend, I mean, why was she a no show?"

"She told me that her kid became ill, and her mom strongly suggested that she stay home with her sick child. And so, that's what she did. As a mother, myself, I ain't mad at her for that!"

"Okay, so, do you think Serena knew what kind of party this was?"

"No, I seriously doubt it!"

"Well, I'm gonna need you to give me all the information you have regarding your friend. We're gonna have to bring her in for questioning."

"Fine!" She looked at the window behind the Sargent. "Is that one of those two-way mirrors, like you see on all those tv cop shows?" She got up and head over toward the glass window, looking into it as if her eyes pierced straight through to the people in the surveillance room.

"What are you doing?" Perkins asked.

He continued, "Ma'am, I'm gonna need you to keep your seat, please."

Natasha kept walking. She approached the surveillance window. Gazing into the glass, "Is the owner back there watching and listening? Good! I just want him to know, yes... I was there, and yes... I guess that makes me a trespasser. So, if you feel you need to press charges against me, lock me up, take away my job and possibly my child, well, I guess that's your legal right. I just want you to know that I had no idea of the kind of event this was. I promise you I would never knowingly take part in something like that!"

Natasha's suspicions were correct. Lee and a couple detectives were in the surveillance room, watching and listening. Detective Hartman said to Lee, "Well, the ball's in your court, what do you want to do?" Lee responded,

"I don't see any point in pressing charges against her. The way I see it, she was just an innocent person who happened to be in the wrong place at the wrong time. Now, the guys who orchestrated this whole thing, well... they're the ones I want!"

CHAPTER 14

CALL FOR THE TEAM

About midday, at home in her daughter's room, Michelle sat on the bed reading a letter from Lindsey who was now away on a college tour. In the letter, Lindsey told her mom how much she loved the place and so far, she felt pretty sure that this was where she wanted to further her education. She mentioned that a few of her high school friends were there, as well, and that they would be joining other tour groups on a camping trip. She also mentioned that there will be guys present, but the girls have their cabins and the guys have theirs, which was in a completely different area, and the whole event would be well-chaperoned. She ended the letter to her mom, "I can just imagine what you may have been wondering about, but I can assure you, that I have my head on straight. I'm focused. So, put your mind at ease. Love you mom. See you soon. Hugs and kisses, Lindsey."

The letter brought a smile to Michelle's face as she was delighted to hear from her daughter, and to know that all was well, and that she was enjoying herself.

The doorbell rang. She went to answer the door and found no one there. She stepped outside to look around, and still, there was no one in sight. Turning back to reenter the house, she found a note stuck to the door that read, "Watching you. Watching your daughter too."

Michelle rushed back into the bedroom to get her cell phone to call and check on her daughter. Before she could make the call, the doorbell rang a second time. Again, she went to answer the door, but this time she was not exactly alone or vulnerable.

Expecting trouble, Michelle came to the door with a gun in her hand. Lee, noticing the door about to come open, was somewhat excited as he was expecting a joyful reunion. However, his joyful spirit was immediately canceled out, by a great deal of caution, as he noticed the gun that Michelle was holding. "Hey, whoa, what's this? What's going on?"

Michelle, very much relieved and delighted to find Lee standing there, said, "Sorry! Come on in. I thought you might be one of those guys from the party incident."

"Really? They've been hassling you?"

"It just started. Just a few minutes before you showed up, someone rang my doorbell. When I came to answer the door, there was no one there. They left this note on the door." She handed the note to Lee. He read the note. Somewhat puzzled, Lee said to Michelle, "How the hell did they even link you to this?" He asked.

"On the night of the party, as I was giving information to one of the officers, a guy rode by staring right at me as he passed. I should have alerted the officer right then, I guess... but my mind was on Paula and her well-being.

70

And now, those thugs are targeting me. And, even worse, they're targeting my daughter. I should call Lindsey."

Michelle was just about to call her daughter.

"Wait! Maybe not," Lee said, "I'm pretty sure the news of this would absolutely ruin her tour experience. She could never enjoy herself for worrying about your safety as well as her own. I have a better idea." Lee took out his cell phone and scrolled through the contacts.

"Who are you calling?" Michelle asked.

"This game they're playing, it's nothing new. Trust me, your daughter will be fine, and so will you, I'm gonna see to that!" Lee made a call to his friend, "Hey, Bobby." Michelle listened as Lee chatted on the phone. "Yeah, it's me... that's right! You know I'm good but listen... Indianapolis needs us." In agreement with his buddy on the phone, Lee continued, "Yeah, oh Yeah... just like that... Good deal! I'll see you then." Lee assured Michelle that everything was under control.

Briefing with Congressman Carrington

Tuesday morning, Lee and Michelle arrived downtown Indianapolis at the capitol building. The two head to a board room where they met with Congressman Andrew Carrington and a few of his associates. This was not a lengthy meeting, but rather a briefing for the upcoming meeting with the mayor, and other city and state officials, that was to take place on the very next day.

"So, today I just wanted to have a brief moment here to meet with you guys and to let you know that I've gone ahead and set up a meeting among a few city and state officials for later this evening. The idea is to try and get them on board, at least, as far as to convince them to listen to your pitch. You need not be present for that, but assuming that it all goes well, I'd like to have you guys right back here tomorrow to actually make your pitch to the mayor. Walt has filled me in, quite a bit on what it is you're trying to accomplish," Carrington said.

"And you must think we're crazy, huh?" Lee asked.

"Oh no, not at all, actually, I commend you on your desire for change… real change," Carrington said.

"But?"

"But… change as significant as what you're proposing is definitely going to require certain key elements. The first would be guts, which I've heard, that you both have plenty of." Michelle, taking a quick smirk look at Lee,

"At least one of us does."

"Oh, I would say both," Carrington said, "And secondly… would be connections. And I'll be happy to assist you with that part."

"Great!" Lee peeped at his watch, realizing that Bobby and the team should be landing shortly, "I always say… big plans… need big connections." Getting up to leave, Lee continued, "well, I guess that about does it for now. I hope your next meeting goes well, and tomorrow… we'll be ready to make that pitch."

CHAPTER
15

Arrival of The Team

A plane lands at the Indianapolis airport. A group of men and women gathered at the carousel to retrieve their luggage. Each member of this group was capable of portraying many different characters. The group exited the building with their luggage. After a short wait, they boarded a small transporter which took them over to the car rental area. They rented three cars and departed traveling four to a car. Riding along, Bobby contacted Lee on his cell. He got the info on Serena Collins as they discuss a strategy to disarm and capture Frank and his gang of thugs.

Later in the day at a popular shopping mall, in downtown Indianapolis, Serena Collins sat in a popular shoe store, trying on a pair of heels. Not so comfortable with the fit, she asked the associate for a larger size.

The sales associate went to the stock room to check for the size requested. Still fumbling with the shoe, Serena heard a male voice, "Excuse me, ma'am, I hope you don't mind a compliment because those cutouts look really nice on you."

"Really? You think so?"

"Absolutely!"

"Well, thank you!"

"You're certainly welcome."

"I see you know a little bit about shoes, huh?"

"Yeah," Bobby said, "you might say that I know a little bit about shoes. After all, I only invested in about a dozen stores across the country. So yeah, I guess you could say that I know a little bit about shoes, huh."

"A dozen stores... wow!" Serena looked around, "So, where is Mrs. shoe store investor?"

Bobby responded jokingly, by also looking around, "There is no Mrs. shoe store investor."

"So how did I get so lucky as to meet such a well to do entrepreneur like yourself?" Serena asked.

"By trying on one of our best brands." Bobby replied.

"So, is this one of your stores... or one that you're invested in?"

"Not this one in particular. The folks here wouldn't know me from Adam, but they do carry a few of our brands, that is... the brands that I've invested in."

"So, you just happened to drop in to check on your brands, is that it?"

"Well, not exactly. Truth is... I saw you come in, and I couldn't help but notice your very fashionable sense of style. I was just curious to see what brand you would choose. And sure enough... you chose one of our best sellers. And that makes me very happy!"

"You know, I never would have thought of the fact that my shoe buying could make a man so happy."

"Well, from an investor's standpoint... I can just imagine that all your years of shoe buying has probably made, not only a lot of men happy, but, a lot of female investors, very happy as well."

"Hmm! Suddenly, I'm starting to feel like… I just might be doing you a favor, in buying these shoes."

"A favor? Now, that's an original thought! I've never heard anyone suggesting that buying something, for themselves, could actually be a favor to someone else."

"Well, looking at the big picture… that's kind of how I see it. I mean, what's in it for me?"

"Well, you get to look good in the shoes," Bobby said.

"Yeah, that's all fine and good, but I'm just saying… kind of feels like I should be getting a little more out of this deal," Serena said.

"Oh, we have a deal now, do we? So, what would you like… an outfit or something to go with those shoes?"

"That… or two or three would be nice!"
They shared a light-hearted laugh.

"You know what, you are something else, you know that? But I like you," Bobby said.

"I like you too," She responded.

"Tell you what," Bobby said, "how about, we start over with an introduction and perhaps a dinner on me." He stretched forth his hand, "Hi, I'm Bobby. So nice to meet you?" She took his hand, "Serena! And it's nice to meet you as well. Now, where we gonna eat?"

Later that evening at Michelle's house, Lee sat in the living room on the sofa, talking on his cell phone to Bobby, who was now driving, in route to pick up Serena for dinner. Into the phone, Lee asked, "So, is she singing or what?"

"Haven't got that far yet. I thought it best to take it kind of slow, so as not to make her suspicious. We'll be having dinner tonight." A bit surprised, "dinner?" Lee asked.

"Yeah, that way I'll be able to get her to loosen up and start talking. I'm on my way to pick her up right now."

"Alright. Well, I know I don't have to ask, but… you are focused on the task at hand, right?" Lee asked. "Absolutely!"
Lee continued, "And you will get the goods, right?"

"Oh, I'm gonna get the goods!" Bobby replied.
Lee looked as though he recognized a bit of subtext there,

but without commenting on it, "Well, don't take too long, we gotta move on this!"

Following the call, he made to Lee, Bobby made another call to update the team, "Hey Jack, how's everything going there, everybody good?"

"It's all good here. Everybody's ready to do what we came to do!"

"Good. So, look... I'm gonna need a few bodies in place at a joint called, uh..." He took out a piece of paper that he had written a name on. "...ARCHIE'S. It's supposed to be a popular spot. There, I think we might find some of the guys we are looking for."

Bobby arrived at Serena's place. He rang the doorbell. Serena answered the door wearing the shoes that he had ended up buying for her when they first met at the mall.

"Well, look at you! You look absolutely stunning tonight. If there ever were a, as you put it, Mrs. shoe store owner or investor, I don't think she'd be very happy right now. I mean, just look at you. Tonight, you look absolutely irresistible."

"I'll bet you say something like that to all the ladies, but that's okay though. I can appreciate a little bit of flattery. And who knows... it just might get you somewhere."
He smiled, "Shall we go?"

"Certainly!"
They head to the car. Like a gentleman, Bobby got the door for the lady and off they went.

At Michelle's house, Lee was still sitting on the sofa checking messages on his cell phone. The TV was on at a low volume. Michelle was in the kitchen fixing a snack for Lee and herself. Coming in from the kitchen, Michelle entered the living room, with a bowl of fruit and whipped cream. She took a seat on the sofa beside Lee. "What are you watching on TV?"

"Nothing really," he said, "it's just on."

"So, tell me about those associates of yours."

"Not much to tell, really. Let's just say that... they are a courageous group of people who happen to be very good at

76

handling just about any kind of situation that may arise. And they... we... all share a common cause."

"And that cause is?" Michelle asked.

"Righting the wrongs of society." Lee replied.

"Well, you must know that one might consider such a group to be nothing more than a bunch of vigilantes."

"You say... one might... I say... several might! The truth is we're just good people trying to do the right thing," Lee said.

"So let me get this straight, you want me not to contact the police, but instead, just sit idly by, and do nothing, while those thugs out there take aim at me and my daughter, trusting that your so-called 'good people' will keep us safe?"

"Listen, I understand how you feel."
Michelle stopped him, "Do you? Really? Do you have a teenage daughter?"
Lee tried to respond, "No, but I--," Michelle cut him off,

"Well, how the hell... could you possibly understand how I feel!"

"All I'm trying to say... is that... if I did have a daughter... and I've received a letter, note, phone call, or any kind of threat against her safety or well-being, I would want to employ the fastest form of protection possible. That's what you get with this team. And as far as it goes with the police, no disrespect intended... but the way they operate, as much as I hate to say... by the time they actually get there... it could be too late for your daughter. She could end up being brought out in a body bag. So, listen... right now, even as we speak, the team already has people in place. Lindsey is safe, and so are you. I told you I would see to that, and I have. So, let's not jeopardize her safety or ruin her experience, with police involvement just yet. This team is very good at what it does, so just let them do what they do. And trust me, the bad guys will be caught and turned over to the police soon enough."

Michelle, who had been trying to hold it together since the beginning, dropped her head as she weakened into a state of mild weeping. Lee put his arms around Michelle to comfort her. Michelle said, "I'm sorry, I didn't mean to flare up at you. I guess I just became a bit overwhelmed with all of this. Sometimes I feel like… I just wish it was all over, you know?"

"Yes… I know! And don't worry about the flare-up… I get it! But we must continue the fight for Paula's sake, and for the sake of all the other innocent victims whose lives have been taken, due to all of the ruthless gun violence that's taking place across the nation. But for now, just try to relax. And don't worry… it'll all work out, you'll see!"

CHAPTER 16

Bobby Meets Frank

At Archie's Bar and Grill, Bobby and Serena were seated in a booth opposite one another, with menus in hand. Associates, of both Bobby and Frank, were present and positioned throughout the place, but only Bobby's guys were aware of the situation at hand.

The server came to take drink orders for Bobby and Serena, "Hi, guys. Welcome to Archie's. I'm Sherri and I'll be your server. It's margarita night, which means all of our margaritas are half-priced."

"Now that's what I'm talking about. Girl, this is my kind of night! I'll have a frozen strawberry margarita."

"And for you, sir?" The server asked.

"Well… let's see now… tell you what… I'll try your favorite… whatever that may be."

"Good choice. I'll be right back."

Serena gave Bobby a strange look, "Well, aren't you just the smooth operator."

"What?" with a grin, Bobby asked.

"What!... You know what! I see I'm gonna have to keep my eye on you... that's what!"

Bobby took a quick visual assessment of the surroundings, after which, he turned his attention back to Serena.

"So, this is your favorite spot, huh?"

"Well, I don't know if I would say absolute favorite, but definitely one of them."

"Ah! One of your favorites. Okay, well it seems like a good choice so far," Bobby said.

"Yeah, a lot of friends, co-workers, and associates come here."

"Partygoers?" Bobby inquired.

"Oh Yeah! Goers and throwers!"

"Sounds interesting." Now that he had her talking, he figured it was time, to start digging, to get the scoop on Frank and his gang. "Well, by all means, do tell... give me the lay of the land." Completely off course, Serena responds, "Wait a minute! You better not be trying to use me to pick up other women up in here, now!"

"No-no-no! Why would I do that... when I'm already with the most beautiful woman in here? I just always find it kind of interesting to get to know who's who, that's all!"

"That's all, huh! Well... Better be!"

He held up two fingers, "Scout's honor!"

"Okay, scout's honor... I don't even know if that's the correct sign or not!" Unaware of what she was actually doing, Serena continued, pointing out members of Franks gang, "Anyway..." as she looked to the area behind Bobby and off to his right, "See the chick over there with the blond weave... goer!" She looked to another area, "See the chick over there with the long braids... goer! The four in the booth over here to my left... all goers! Now, the three guys over at the bar... definitely throwers!

And the guy over there on the phone, surrounded by all those young ladies, is the big baller, shot caller... Frank Manning. Most just call him THE MAN." Frank was on the phone with Watch Boy, who was hiding at the campsite on assignment to kidnap Lindsey. He was waiting for her to turn in, as he planned to nab her while she slept. Frank spoke into the phone with his cool lingo, "Hey, Watch Boy, just checking on you baby, making sure everything is going as planned."

Responding from his vantage point at the campsite, as he peered through a pair of binoculars, enjoying what he was seeing, "Yeah man, everything here's looking real fine. Right now, everybody's just running around laughing and having a good time. They should be getting ready, to go back to their cabins pretty soon, to wind down. I'll give her a few minutes to get into a deep sleep, then I'll snatch her little fine ass up and be back at the spot before daylight."

"Whoa-whoa-whoa! Slow your roll, now! Don't get sidetracked. Just do your job baby. And Watch Boy... don't spoil the goods!" Frank said, before ending the call.

The server returned to the table with drinks for Bobby and Serena. She sat the drinks before them. Serena, wasting no time indulging, "Mmm... so good!"

"Well, looks like I have the same thing." Bobby said. Giving Bobby somewhat of a flirtatious look, the server said, "Yeah, turns out she and I seem to like the same thing!" Bobby smiled, "Well, how about that!" Serena looked at Bobby, "Yeah... how about that!"

"So, are we ready to order?" The server asked. They made their selections, and the server went to put in their order.

Frank stopped by their table as he and his girls were on their way out. He spoke to Serena, "Hey, baby girl! How you been? We missed you at the party a few weeks ago."

"Yeah, sorry I couldn't make it, I was dealing with some issues that night."

"I see," Frank said. He looked at Bobby, "Now, would this be one of your issues?"

"No-no, nothing like that!"

There was a slight tension building between Bobby and Frank. Serena made an introduction to ease the tension.

"Frank, this is Bobby! He's an investor. Bobby, this is Frank! He's a producer."

"Ah! Producer! Music, movies?" Bobby asked.

"Events!" Frank responded.

Breaking the tension again, Serena said to Frank, "And you be sure to let me know about the next one, now!"

"You know I will. I'll be in touch. Nice to meet you, investor Bobby."

"Likewise… though I never really thought of myself as being anybody's issue!"

"Hey… just having a little fun with you, baby!" He said to Serena, "Oh, and uh, speaking of issues… you might just be glad you didn't make it to that party. You may have heard… we had quite an issue of our own to deal with that night."

"Well, I'm sure it was nothing you couldn't handle."

"Sho-you-right! In fact, part of it's being handled even as we speak!"

The Campsite

Back at the campsite, as it got late into the night, some of the youngsters remained sitting around the campfire laughing and having a good time. Some of the campers retreated to their cabins while others pay visits to their friend's cabin.

Watch Boy had already scoped out the place earlier. He had found his vantage point before the girls arrived at the camp. He knew which cabin Lindsey belonged to. He had watched the girls as they unpacked. He now knew which bed was Lindsey's, and which bed was her roommate's.

Though everyone was currently having fun running around throughout the campsite, Watch Boy kept a close eye on Lindsey's cabin from afar.

After patiently waiting, finally, he saw two young ladies enter the cabin. As the two young ladies prepared for bed, he enjoyed watching them as they changed out of their clothes and into their sleepers. After a good while, he decided that the time was right to make his move.

Watch Boy left his vantage point, eased over and into Lindsey's cabin. On the right side of the room, a female figure lay in bed with the covers pulled completely up and over her head. Knowing that Lindsey's bed was on the left, he looked at the figure of the body lying in her bed, which was also completely covered from head to toe.

Watch Boy took out a cloth that had been douched in chloroform. He intended to ease back the covers, just enough to expose Lindsey's face, so that he may render her unconscious. He knew that otherwise, she would surely try to put up a fight, to avoid being kidnapped.

As Watch Boy was about to grab the covers, he noticed some movement taking place underneath. This causes him to pause for a moment. He paid attention to the movement and realized that it was a slow but steady repetition. He lost focus of his mission as he thought he knew what was going on under the covers. Watch Boy became overwhelmed by his own imagination. Excited about what he thought he would see, he snatched the covers off of her body and was shocked, times three, by what he discovered.

First, he was greeted by a nine-millimeter handgun that was pointed right at him.

Secondly, he realized that the young lady lying there was not Lindsey. The young lady with the gun was actually Amanda, a member of Bobby's team, who said "Well, now don't look so surprised, we've been expecting you!"

"We?" Watch Boy asked.

The third shock that Watch Boy received was the realization that the covered body in the bed on the right was not Lindsey's roommate, as Jackie, another member of Bobby's team got up putting a gun to the back of his head, said, "that's right… we!"

He realized that he had been outsmarted by these ladies and now found himself at their mercy.

83

The two ladies had been stationed at the campsite as part of Lee and Bobby's plan. They had already arranged to have board games in progress at one of the other cabins.

The games had been perfectly timed, to ensure that both, Lindsey and her roommate would be safely out of the way, in another cabin. As the girls enjoyed a night of fun and games, they were unaware of Frank's plan to have Watch Boy, kidnap Lindsey and bring her to the clubhouse.

Watch Boy stood helpless, still holding the chloroform cloth in his hand, as he received instructions from Jackie.

"Now just take that rag, and put it over your own nose, and breathe deep... real deep!"

Watch Boy realized that he didn't have a chance. Standing there between two guns, he figured he'd better comply. He put the cloth to his face and began to take deep breaths. It didn't take very long for him to collapse.

The two ladies tied Watch Boy up and took him to a car, that was staged, just a little ways off from the camp. They stuffed him into the trunk and took him back to Frank's clubhouse, where they would continue their plot, to outfox Frank and his gang.

CHAPTER

17

Meeting at The Indiana State Capital Building

(Second Pitch)

Early Wednesday morning, Lee and Michelle arrived at the Capitol Building. They pulled into a parking space.

"So, how do you think this is going to go?" Michelle asked.

"Not sure, but there's only one way to find out," Lee said.

They head on inside the Capitol Building. They pass through the security checkpoint, and onto the meeting room.

Once inside, they see Congressman Andrew Carrington, Indianapolis mayor, Jim Hogan, and a few other city and state officials, who were already seated.

Carrington got up out of his seat to greet Lee and Michelle as they entered the room, "Alright, there they are, our diehard crime fighters." He extended his hand to Lee, "good to see you!"

Lee responded, as he shook Carrington's hand, "Likewise! If nothing else… I guess we've at least earned a name for ourselves, huh?"

"And a good one at that!" Carrington said.

He also shook Michelle's hand. "And how are you doing today?"

"Fine, thank you!" Michelle responded.

"So, I believe you guys have met, or at least know everyone here."

Lee, speaking for them both, "Yes. Ladies! Gentlemen!" Michelle smiled and nodded her head with a speaking gesture.

They all took their seats. "So, here's where we are," Carrington said, "as you know some of us got together yesterday and met with a host of city and state officials, some of whom could not be present today, and the overall consensus, though not necessarily all of our views individually, was that this whole idea would rock the boat a little too hard."

Lee responded to Carrington's comment, "See now that's a big part of the problem. We've got a bunch of elected officials just sitting idle in a freaking boat that's already full of holes, and all they seem to be worried about is not rocking the damn thing, when the focus should really be about trying to figure out, how the hell to fix it! How the hell do we plug the holes!"

Carrington responded, "Well, I don't know about the sitting idle part, but I get it. I understand and agree with your interesting metaphor."

"Actually, it was yours… I just expanded upon it."

"Right, but that's where we are, and I wish there was more we could do!"

"You know what," Lee said, "maybe I went about this all wrong. Maybe I came on a little too strong, talking about possibly making changes to the Constitution of the United States of America. Maybe that scared the hell out of a lot of your constituents. Perhaps, I should have started by unveiling some of the more involved details of this whole idea. If this whole thing was presented as a bill, we might call it something like… 'The Crime Fix Bill.' And perhaps it could have a few subtitles that mention things like: Gun Reform, Gun Sense, Gun Smart, or Gun Control, even! And yes… I'm very much aware of how some groups feel about certain titles or choice of words. I understand the need to appear politically correct sometimes causes them to tread lightly or dance around certain issues. But regardless, what language you choose to use, metaphorically speaking, when it comes to fixing the holes in this particular boat… the ones that are claiming the lives of far too many innocent victims… Gun Control is where we need to start!"

State official, David Pena said to Lee, "All due respect, there's already been plans and programs put in place to combat the problems with gun control, or the lack thereof."

"All due respect, how's that working out? I'm talking about something that will absolutely, positively work! This idea will save a lot of lives. So, let me ask you this, how many of you are married?" Everyone raised their hands except Lee and Michelle. He continued, "Just about everyone, great! And how many of you have kids?" To this question, even Lee and Michelle's hand went up along with everyone else's. He continued, "Okay, very good, just trying to make sure that you all have people in your lives, who matter to you, and you feel that their lives are worth saving.

Now, as you know, people are being gunned down in the streets, in their homes, on their jobs, at school, at the movies, at concerts, at sporting events, and even in the church, of all places.

I present to you something that will put an end to a whole lot of the gun violence that's taking place around the nation. So, at this time, Michelle will reveal some of the details of this proposal. But, let me just kind of forewarn you, it is deep. In fact, some of you may even view it as extreme. But remember this... it will work!"

He called Michelle. Michelle began to speak, "A license to carry. Instead of--"

Lee jumped back in cutting her off, "Excuse me a minute, sorry... but I gotta weigh in on that. A license... Really? That in itself has become a freaking joke! How many criminals out there murdering people in the streets, every freaking day, do you think actually have a license to carry? They don't give a damn about a license. Even if they had one... that alone wouldn't prevent them from murdering a bunch of innocent people."

All eyes stared at Lee because he had become quite intense as he rendered his comments. "Sorry... please go ahead," He said to Michelle, "Guess I got a little worked up, huh?"

"A little!" She responded.

Michelle continued to speak to the officials, "So, anyway... we're not suggesting that we do away with the licensing process. But what we are saying... is instead of just relying on its false sense of security, instead of relying on the building of a few neighborhood youth centers, and instead of relying on a bunch of sign-yielding protesters... let's consider something that will really make a difference. Now, just to kind of forewarn you, as Lee mentioned earlier, what I'm about to share with you is kind of deep. You will likely need to study it a bit. After doing so, I'm sure you will see that this would be a really good solution to our gun control problem."

Michelle flipped open her notes and began to read some of the details of their idea. "We have an idea, called the Gunsmart System, which utilizes a three-piece combination of electronic equipment. **First**, would be the **Firearm Chip (FC)**. **Second**, would be the **Armband Communicator (AC)**. And **third**... the **Stationary Base Unit** (SBU), which could be installed in residential, commercial, and public locations. Each piece of equipment would be chipped and trackable. Also, each piece of equipment would feed information into a centralized database. All data would be received, analyzed, and responded to accordingly, by the proper authorities. The armband communicator (AC), which would be much like that of an apple watch, could have a minimum six-digit passcode made up of both letters and numbers. The armband communicator (AC) should always accompany the firearm, with a maximum separation, extending no more than five feet, anytime there is movement of the firearm, by more than one foot. If this condition is not satisfied, the infraction would be communicated to the central database. The owner of the firearm would then be prompted to send the correct code. Anytime the firearm travels beyond forty yards of the stationary base unit (SBU) the owner will be prompted to send the correct code. From a predetermined distance, the (SBU) would recognize the presence of both the (FC) and the (AC) prior to the entry of any type of dwelling. When away from the stationary base unit (SBU), the armband communicator (AC) must remain within five feet of the firearm, otherwise you'll be prompted to send a code. The (SBU) would be equipped with adjustable perimeter settings, only to be set by the proper authorities.

All distances previously mentioned, are suggestions only, and should ultimately be determined by the proper authorities.

All firearms must be registered. If any piece of equipment is damaged, tampered with, or should malfunction, the owner would be prompted to send the code or call in to the central database.

If no code, or wrong code, is received after being prompted to send, authorities will be dispatched. Authorities could also be dispatched anytime a firearm is discharged, if not previously notified, depending on circumstances. When visiting a gun range, authorities must be notified before your visit. Authorities must also be notified prior to any type of hunting or gun sporting events."

The look on some of the faces of the people in the room seemed to show a sincere interest. Some even seemed to show signs of absolute favor, while others seemed to show early signs of opposition. Michelle continued, "We could implement random inspections, consisting of vehicular traffic, pedestrian traffic, public dwellings, and yes, even residential and business dwellings. All communicators and chips would contain identification info. Any person caught, with a firearm that has no chip, or chip that doesn't match the armband communicator, (AC), or they have no armband communicator, that person would be arrested. This system would surely save a lot of time and tax dollars, due to a huge reduction in investigative efforts. No more trying to figure out who did what, when, or where."

State official, Howard Pearson said, "You know... I've served in this position I think longer than anyone here in this room. Believe me when I say... I've seen many bills and ideas presented, in my time. Some get put into action and perform quite well just as intended. Others are short-lived and thrown out after being summed up as a waste of time, money, and effort. And then, there are those that never receive enough consideration to ever become a reality at all. But I must say... I think you may actually be on to something here!"

"Yeah, well that's all fine and dandy, I mean, be that as it may... even if we were to agree on pushing this whole idea as a bill for gun control, how do you suppose we go about implementing such an operation, and how do you suppose we go about paying for it all?" David Pena asked.

"Well, actually, I believe that the financial part of the solution should be worked out by our elected officials. But I will say this… it's been reported that investigative efforts involving gun violence, is costing the American public approximately seven hundred dollars per person, annually. Now, if you calculate that out, I believe you'll find that in a city such as Indianapolis, with an estimated population of about eight hundred sixty-nine thousand, the total estimated cost would be over six hundred million dollars. I'm thinking that… just maybe, if we were to reallocate some of those funds, perhaps that would go a long way toward implementing such an operation," Lee explained.

"So, you come up with this whole bright idea about gun control… but when it comes to the hard part such as financing, then you just lay it all in our laps, is that it?" David asked.

"Well, when it comes to things like; building new stadiums, art galleries, ice rinks, or water parks and other projects, somehow… the money is always found. So, if saving the lives of your loved ones, or even possibly that of your own, is as important as any of the things I've just mentioned, you'll find a way. You always do! But make no mistake about it… this my friend is a very real solution for gun control, or rather… the lack thereof."

Lee rolled up a piece of paper and said, "If this were a mic, I'd drop it right here!" He dropped the paper, which symbolized the dropping of a microphone.

Indianapolis Mayor, Jim Hogan, said to Lee, "You seem to have all the answers. Perhaps you should run for office."

"No thanks! Politics ain't my thing," Lee responded. David said, "I understand there's been some kind of vigilante activity, if you will… that--"
Lee cut him off sharply, "I won't!"

"Excuse me?"

"I will not refer to the people, that I believe you're speaking of, as vigilantes."

"Well then, how would you categorize them?" David asked.

"Just a good group of people, with a good common interest," Lee said.

"And that interest being, what?" David asked.

"A nationwide crime fix, starting with gun control, starting right here in Indianapolis," Lee replied.

David leaned back in his seat. "So, just force people to conform to your line of thinking. Wow! Now that sounds a lot like The Donald!"

"You know… like it or not, The Donald is quite a clever person. He's serious, he's strong, and he's courageous. I like that in a man. My hat goes off to the guy. Now, I'm not exactly saying that I agree with everything he says or does, but the guy does have some characteristics that I can definitely respect."

City Official Eileen Thompson weighs in, "Somehow, that doesn't surprise me. But you know this whole idea could be viewed as an infringement against one's civil rights. Considering The People… I just can't imagine that for the most part they would be willing to give up any of their civil liberties, especially when it comes to their right to privacy, not to mention their right to bear arms."

"It's not like we're suggesting that the government install cameras in every home in the nation and monitor them twenty-four seven. Now that would be a total invasion of privacy. Instead, under this plan, you could be checked today and not have another inspection for the next five or six years, or… on the other hand, you could be checked again two days later. That's random and that's what makes random work. Otherwise, if they were notified of an upcoming inspection, you tell me what criminal would not hide all of their illegal possessions, until after it was over? Random works… people! I've known this for decades. Because, for decades I've dealt with the Department of Transportation, and for decades they've been conducting random inspections. Believe me when I tell you… random inspections always yield great results! What else can I say? It works!

So, you see, this doesn't take away anyone's right to privacy, nor does it take away anyone's right to bear arms. What it does, is drastically reduce the potential, not only to commit murder, but also, to get away with it. And, as far as the citizens right to bear arms, this plan does not take away that right, instead, it enhances it," Lee said.

"We've compiled a list of scenarios, all of which are based on real-life occurrences. I believe it will be quite helpful in convincing the people that this is the right thing," Michelle mentioned.

"The right thing?" David asked.

Michelle responded, "At least, a very good thing! We'll be presenting this idea at a neighborhood meeting this coming Saturday. I would encourage you all to attend. That way, we all get a first-hand look at just how well this would all go over with The People. And if in fact, this does go well, perhaps you'll meet with other city officials and try to implement this idea throughout the state, and at some point... the nation."

"A neighborhood meeting... Saturday... The People's response. Well, why not? This I'd love to see," Mayor Hogan said.

After the meeting ended, Carrington called Lee and Michelle to the side, "Excuse me, I'd like to speak with you guys for just a moment. You may not realize this... but the position I took just a few minutes ago in the meeting was the best thing for the moment. You see... I like what you're saying, and I believe your ideas are worth being heard on a larger scale. So, I thought it best not to stir the pot too deeply at this point. Better to give your ideas a chance to ease forward and grab the attention of more power players nationwide. I know a lot of people in key positions all across the nation. I'm talking about people who I believe would be in favor of your proposal. Getting these people on board, will surely give your ideas a better chance of survival as a bill... and possibly being implemented into law.

So, I'll be happy to assist you, by contacting these people to set up meetings in many of the nation's hot spots. That is, of course… if you're up for it," Carrington said.

"We are," Lee replied.

He looked at Michelle. She responded, "Yes… Absolutely! We are!"

"Great! Now, I may not be able to be with you at some of these meetings, but I trust you'll put your best foot forward and make a strong pitch. For now, I'm only speaking to you guys about all of this. So, just keep this conversation under your hat until I get everything set up. I'll be in touch!"

CHAPTER 18

Frank Being Duped

On the same day, while Lee and Michelle met with city and state officials at the State House, back at frank's clubhouse in an upper room, Amanda and Jackie have Watch Boy tied up, gagged, and bound to a chair. Amanda had possession of Watch Boy's phone, as they wait for Frank to try and make contact. A text comes in, it's Frank, checking to see if everything was going as planned. Amanda, looking at the phone and seeing that it's Frank, said to Watch boy, "Well, it's about time your boy Frank decided to check up on you." She read the text out loud, "What's up boy! I'll be stopping by shortly to check on things. You do have the girl, right?"

Pretending to be Watch Boy, Amanda spoke out loud while texting him back, "Yeah, I got her. Everything's all secure. She ain't going nowhere!"

Making sure that their plans go smoothly when Frank arrived, Jackie had used a syringe to further silence Watch Boy before tucking him away. Amanda asked Jackie, "Are you sure you gave him enough to keep him quiet?"

"Don't worry about him, he'll be out for a good long while," Jackie said.

The ladies went back down to the big open room on the first floor. Amanda sat in a chair in the middle of the room. Jackie tied her up, but in such a way that she could easily free herself if need be.

Accompanied by three of his goons, Frank sat in the back seat of a sedan, in route to the clubhouse. The guys arrived at the clubhouse. Jackie went and hid, with a vast array of weaponry, ready to respond, should the situation start to get out of hand. Frank had never seen Lindsey before, nor does he have any idea what she looked like. They entered and found Amanda, seemingly, bound to a chair in the middle of the room. They were being duped into thinking that Amanda was, Michelle's daughter, Lindsey. They thought that Watch boy had done well by kidnapping Lindsey and bringing her to be held hostage there at the clubhouse. As far as Frank could tell, his plan was on point.

Thinking that he was speaking to Lindsey, Frank said, "Well-well-well, if it ain't little miss crimefighter's daughter. How you doing, baby girl?" She responded in a very hostile and sarcastic manner, "How am I doing? Well, in case you haven't noticed... I'm a little tied up at the moment!"

"Yeah, well... I'm really sorry about that," Frank said.

"uh-huh, sure you are!"

"But that's the way it's gotta be. I gotta get through to your mom, to have her and that boyfriend of hers call off this little quest of theirs before they mess up a good thing."

"For one... my mother doesn't have a boyfriend..."

"Now, that's a damn shame!

Maybe I should have had her fine ass brought here, instead of you, huh?

"You couldn't handle my mom! And another thing... you call this little operation of yours a good thing... well I say, you and good, don't mix!"

"Well, sure it does, baby girl. You see good are the guns that I have, to protect myself and my business. So, you see... my guns are good for me, but not so much for my adversaries. You see... I know that the cops have been hauling people in downtown trying to get the low down on me and my operation. So, that's why I need to get your mom's attention and get her to back the hell off. I've heard about some of the gun control ideas that she and that partner of hers have been putting in the minds of the people. She and some of her politician friends along with these damn cops are creating a stink that could jeopardize my whole operation. Make no mistake about it... I don't intend to just sit back and let that happen."

Frank leaned in close and softly stroked her cheek with the back of his hand.

"But don't you worry that pretty little body of yours. Ain't nobody gonna hurt you." She spat at him. He was quick to turn his face. Her spit landed on the side of his cheek. He remained calm as he wiped the spit from his face.

"You're upset... It's understandable. Watch Boy didn't try to bother you, did he?"

Frank looked around and, not seeing Watch Boy anywhere, asked, "Where is his ass at, anyway?"
Amanda didn't want to blow her cover by having the goons search all over the place. She had to think fast.

"Watch Boy? You mean that dumb ass that brought me here? The same dumbass that went out to waste his money on some damn lottery tickets talking about he's got a feeling he's gonna hit the Big One? Well, I got a feeling too! And my feeling is... that I hope the Big One hit his ass while he's out there. And by the Big One... I mean like a big ass truck, bus, or something.

I hope he never comes back! And you either!" She spat at Frank again, but this time he was able to dodge it.

"You got fire. I like a girl with fire. So, anyway, we gotta run now, but don't you worry about Watch Boy, he'll be back."

Frank and the goons exited the building. Jackie watched carefully from a window on the second floor, as Frank and his guys were about to leave. To make sure that she didn't get out of the chair too soon, Amanda asked Jackie, "Are they gone yet?"

"Not yet," Jackie replied, "I think he's trying to text Watch Boy, or, as you say, 'dumbass.'"

"Hey… had to sell it, right?" Jackie, now with Watch boy's phone, "Yep, and looks like the text is coming in right now." She read the text out loud, for Amanda to hear, "Stopped by to check on the girl. You need to hurry and get your ass back here."

"We better respond to that, huh?" Again, Jackie spoke out loud as she responded to the text, "On my way right now."

The fake news, that Frank received in the text from Jackie, stating that Watch boy was on his way back to attend to the girl, put his mind at ease. He and the guys got into the car and drove off.

CHAPTER 19

The Switch

Posing as an employee of the Imperial Hotel, Jeanie, a member of Bobby's team, goes undercover as a member of guess services. She waited for Frank's arrival. Other members of Bobby's team, who happened to be technologically proficient, had been tailing Frank and his goons for several days, and all the while, had been intercepting all of their phone conversations.

In the car, riding four-deep as always, Frank and the guys pulled up to the hotel. Two members of Bobby's team pulled up behind them, but off at a distance, so as not to be noticed. They phoned ahead to alert Jeanie of Frank's arrival. Before getting out of his car, Frank said to his guys, "So, check it out… this is where I'll be staying, for a few days, while I handle some business. But, tonight, I need you guys back here at eight. Don't be late!" He got out and went inside to check in. His goons left. They still had no idea that they were being followed. Frank got the keys from the front desk and took the elevator to the fifth floor. Once in his room, Frank made a call to his social media guy, "Yo, what's up Turk. Look here baby, the warehouse is a go. I want you to get the word out. I need everybody to be there, alright? I'll be talking to you."

After having dropped Frank off at the hotel, the goons head to a popular strip club. Aware of the club's strict weapons policy as well as their detection devices, the guys hid their guns in the car before going in for a little fun.

The two guys from Bobby's team, who were tailing Frank's goons, waited outside of the club with a close eye on Frank's car. They gave Frank's goons enough time to become immersed in the activities that were taking place on the inside. After a while, Bobby's guys seized the opportunity to get into Frank's car and find the guns, and replaced the real ammunition, with blanks.

Meanwhile, back at the hotel, Frank scrolled through some phone messages. He was about to hit the shower when suddenly there was a knock at the door. Frank went to answer the door and found a beautiful young lady in a hotel uniform standing there with a complimentary fruit basket and a bottle of wine. He was far more interested in the young lady, than the compliments of the hotel.

"Well now... is this my lucky day or what!"
The young lady said, "This is your complimentary package that comes with your room. Just our way of saying thanks for choosing us."

"Oh, I see, a complimentary package, that's great! Well, thank you very much," He looked at her name tag and attempted to pronounce her name, "Miss Sher... Sherlon... Sherlond--" She helped him out, "Sherlonda." Frank repeated after her, "Sherlonda. Oh, okay, that's unique. I've never heard that name before, but I like it! A beautiful name for a beautiful lady." He held up the bottle of wine. "Well then, Miss Sherlonda... would you care to join me?"

Nodding her head, no, "Now you're trying to get me fired."
"No way, baby girl, I wouldn't wanna do that! So, anyway,
I was just about to hit the shower. If by chance you should
change your mind, please feel free to use your master key."

"Well, I'll certainly keep that in mind."
She turned to leave. Frank watched her from behind as she
walked down the hallway. He mumbled to himself, "my-
my-my... Wow!"

Frank went back inside the room. After taking a sip of
wine, he headed for the shower, leaving his gun lying in
plain sight, on a desk near the TV.

After giving Frank enough time to get into the shower,
Sherlonda returned to the room. She found the gun, filled it
with blanks and quickly left the room without his
knowledge.

Meanwhile, back at the strip club, the guys realized that
it was about time to go. They came out of the club and got
into the car. They drove away completely oblivious to the
fact that all of their weapons were now filled with blanks.
They head back to the hotel and waited in the car for Frank
to come out.

Frank came out of the shower and got dressed. He went
to pick up his holster and noticed that the gun strap was not
fastened. He paused to think for a brief moment, as he
found it a little strange. After a few seconds, he shrugged
his shoulders, thinking that perhaps he'd somehow
knocked the strap loose while removing the holster. He
refastened the gun strap, thus making sure that the weapon
would not accidentally fall out. He strapped on the holster,
put on his jacket, and head down to the lobby.

On his way out to meet the guys, Frank stopped by the
front desk to speak to Sherlonda. Noticing Frank as he
approached the counter, "Hey, how was your shower?"
Sherlonda asked.

"All good, baby girl... I mean... Sherlonda. Yeah, it
was all good, but it would have been a lot better had you
decided to come back and join me. We could have made
some really fun memories. You know what I'm saying?"

"Now see, there you go… still trying to get me fired."

"Naw-naw baby, never do that. Besides, if they try to fire you, I will shut this place down. So anyway, I gotta run out now, to a kind of special event. Too bad you're stuck here, I'd love to take you with me, but you got a job to do. Perhaps, I'll see you back here tomorrow or sometime real soon."

"Perhaps! And who knows… maybe even sooner than you think."

Frank received Sherlonda's comment as her being somewhat of a flirt. He had no idea that Sherlonda was, actually Jeanie, a member of Bobby's team. Frank smiled, "Till we meet again."
She returned the smile, "Till we meet again!"

Frank headed out to meet his guys who were waiting in the car. He took his usual seat at the rear passenger side of the vehicle. They pulled off heading to the warehouse that had been converted into a dance club just for this one night.

Seeing that Frank and his goons were gone, Jeanie made a call to Bobby. Bobby's cell phone rang as he and Serena were in route to the warehouse. Bobby answered the phone, "Hello?"

"It's done, the switch has been made and he's on his way to the warehouse," Jeanie said on the other end.

"Very good, glad to hear it. All the others have been taken care of as well. His was the finishing piece. Good job! See you soon!" Bobby ended the call.

"Sounds like business," Serena said.

"Well, what can I say… if you're a businessman or woman, you gotta take care of business, right?"

Frank's car waited for a traffic signal at a busy intersection. A very sharp bike pulled up beside the car on the right side where Frank was sitting. Riding the bike was a very hot chick in a halter top and very short cut-off jeans. Though it was getting late in the evening, the intersection was well lit. The guys in the car marvel at the biker chick's hot body. She wore a helmet with a very dark tinted viewing area.

102

The guys have no idea who was actually on the bike. The guy in the front passenger seat, lowered the window and yelled out as he scanned her body with his eyes, honing-in mostly on her tush, "Damn baby, you got a real nice..." She turned her head to face him, but all he saw was a mysterious looking dark helmet that he could not see into, that seemed to be staring right at him. It chilled him out so much, that he altered his originally intended comment. "...Uh... bike!" The other guys in the car laughed at him. The light turned green. The female biker took off and sped out of sight.

CHAPTER 20

The Big Event

Jeanie, who was the mysterious female biker, arrived at the warehouse in plenty of time to hide the bike. She went inside through a secret passage created by other members of Bobby's team, who had already infiltrated the place. The party was going strong. The place was packed with partygoers. Except for the three guys in the car with Frank, all of his gang members were present. And without their knowledge, all of their guns have been filled with blanks. Frank's car arrived at the warehouse. He and his goons got out and visually scanned the area. They were also packing blanks. Frank was happy to see the many cars, trucks, and bikes, that filled the parking lot.

In Frank's mind, the vast number of vehicles, spelled a large payday for him as he had intended to push a lot of drugs at this event. Frank entered with three of his top guns. Right away, he spotted two of his special guests, who were head of their own gangs. The other two gang leaders would be party to the largest transactions of the night. He went over to chat, "Hey, what's up, baby. So glad y'all could make it. But, uh… looking around, I only see a few of your boys." Gang leader, Double R said, "Well, some of my boys are on another assignment right now, taking care of some important business, you know?"

"Damn right," Frank said, "You know I know! Business first!" Gang leader Big Will responded, "Same thing brother! Besides, we knew you'd have everything under control."

"Believe that!" Frank said.

Bobby and Serena arrived. Before getting out of the car, "Excuse me for just a moment, I have one more piece of business to wrap up really quick," Bobby said.
Serena, having no clue as to what was about to take place, said, "Business-business-business… must be nice to feel so important."

Bobby sent a text to his team, alerting them of his arrival and checking to see that everyone was in place and ready for what was about to go down. He received a confirmation text, that additional members of their team had arrived, and that everyone was in place and ready for action.

"Okay, now that, that's all taken care of, shall we go inside?" Bobby asked.

"We shall!" Serena responded.

Upon entry to the warehouse, they were greeted by Frank, "Well now, baby girl, good to see you coming back to party with us. I see you brought your friend, Billy."

"Bobby!" Bobby said sharply.

"Right, right. Well, look, y'all go and enjoy yourselves, here."

Serena and Bobby had only taken a couple of steps away when Bobby overheard Frank as he spoke to the other two gang leaders, "So look here fellas, uh... I'll get up with y'all in a bit. Gotta make my rounds... check on my boys."
Bobby stopped and turned back to Frank, "Your boys? You mean... like Watch Boy and Randall? They're probably pretty busy right about now."
Frank looked at Serena, "Hold on! What the hell is he talking about?"

"I'm just saying, all these beautiful ladies in here... I can just imagine... that some of your boys may be all tied up right about now." Bobby said.

Frank stepped toward Bobby, "Really? That's what you imagine, huh? Well, you wanna know what I imagine? I imagine that your ass is starting to sound like a damn cop or something! Serena... what the hell's wrong with you... bringing this shit up in here? You know that's gonna cost you!"

"Hold on now... don't go blaming the lady. She doesn't know what's really going on here."

"Really? And how the hell do you know what's going on here? And how the hell you know so much about me and my boys, huh?" Frank asked.

"You'd be surprised by the things I know," Bobby replied.

"Oh yeah? Well, you know what I'm thinking? Yo ass is bout to be surprised to learn your fate right about now!"

Frank raised his hand high into the air and close his fist, signaling for the DJ to stop the music. With his hand still raised, he popped his fingers and several of his goons approached and surrounded Bobby and Serena. Frank spoke to his goons while staring at Bobby, "It appears that we have a suspicious guest. Take him to the spot!" Frank's goons lay hands on Bobby, but before they can take him away, Bobby's team stepped up, with weapons drawn, and outnumbered Frank's guys three to one.

There was a moment of stillness. The air filled with tension, as the two sides stared at one another.

Jeannie, still dressed in her cutoff blue jean shorts and a halter top with the name tag Sherlonda from the hotel pinned on, appeared saying, "Refreshments anyone?" Without noticing who she was, as he was focusing on Bobby and his team, Frank said, "Not now baby girl! We bout to have a--"

Cutting his speech as he recognized her, "hold up! You the chick from the hotel!" He looked at the name tag, "Sherlonda! That was you on the bike! What the hell's going on? What are you doing here?" He looked around, "How many people done got in this mother uninvited, huh? Who was manning the door, and where the hell is Watch Boy?"

Amanda, who Frank thought was Michelle's daughter, Lindsey, and whom he'd last seen tied to a chair back at his clubhouse, appeared. Both he and his goons were shocked to see her. She said to Frank, "Well, you look like you've just seen a ghost. And as for Watch Boy, Bobby was right, you know, he's kind of tied up at the moment." With a remote in her hand, she brought Watch Boy out as he's tied to a battery-operated wheelchair.

Frank, still not realizing that he'd been duped by Amanda, said, "And you that little bitch… Michelle's daughter! See… I told you that you would be safe, and nothing was going to happen to you. But you done gone and messed up now!"

"Actually, no! I'm not Michelle's daughter. I don't know her, and I've never met her. That's just what your dumb ass thought! And as far as messed up goes… it's yo ass that done gone and messed up!"

"Oh yeah?"

"Yeah!"

Frank was fed up. He pulled out his gun, pointing it first at Amanda, but didn't say anything. Next, he put the gun to Watch Boy's head, "How the hell you let this happen, huh?"

"Now-now… don't be so hard on the boy! It's not all his fault," Bobby said.

107

Pointing his gun at Bobby, Frank said, "No?... Then the fault must be yours. I knew there was something I didn't like about your ass when I saw you at Archie's, the other night. I should have iced your ass then!"

"That would have been your best chance," Bobby said.

"Oh yeah?" Frank fired a shot at Bobby.

In a sarcastic manner, Bobby responded by acting as though he'd actually been shot.

Upset at Bobby's performance, Frank fired another shot. He saw that Bobby was unharmed. Puzzled, Frank took a quick look at his gun.

"Aw... what's the matter now? Gun not working so well?" Bobby asked.

Enraged, Frank fired a few more rounds at Bobby.

"Now," Bobby said, "if I were to guess, I would say that you are firing blanks. But that's just it... I don't have to guess... because you are firing blanks!"

"Blanks, huh? Just how the hell did blanks get into my damn gun?" Frank asked. As he looked around at Jeannie and seen the name tag that said Sherlonda, he recalled the encounter he'd had with her back at the hotel. "You! Complimentary package, huh? Well, I got a complimentary package for your ass!" Frank said to his boy, "Jimmy, shoot this bitch! Shoot all these bitches!"

Bobby spoke to Jimmy, "Now hold on there, Mr. Jimmy. You've just seen old Frankie Boy fire off a bunch of rounds at me in front of all these witnesses. Though they were all blanks, he's still gonna be charged with attempted murder. Now, what are you going to do? Are you going to make the same mistake in front of all these witnesses?" Are you going to get yourself an attempted murder charge with a gun that is also filled with blanks?"

Jimmy was hesitant. Frank shouted, "Man shoot that bitch!" Jimmy froze up. Frank snatched the gun from Jimmy and fired it at Bobby. The gun fired nothing but blanks. Frank threw Jimmy's gun to the floor. He grabbed Scotty's gun. Again, he fired at Bobby, and again, all blanks. Frank dropped the gun.

"You're wasting your time and effort," Bobby said, "All of your guns are filled with blanks. Now, as for my team, make no mistake about it… our ammo is very real!"

A few demonstrated by shooting up the bar. People around the bar dove to the floor. Bobby spoke loudly to all of the partygoers, "Now that I have your attention--," His speech got halted by the ringing of his cell phone. He glanced at the phone and seen that the incoming call was from Lee. Before stepping away to have a private phone conversation with Lee, Bobby said to the people, "Excuse me everyone, I gotta take this call. So, I'm gonna need everybody to just hang tight until I return."

CHAPTER

21

The W.A.L.

Bobby answered the phone, "Boss Man!"

Sitting on the sofa at Michelle's house, on the phone, checking on Bobby and the team, Lee asked, "How's everything? Don't sound like much of a party going on."

"Well, we're just having a kind of a quiet moment right now."

"A quiet moment? You don't mean...?"

"Nah... don't I wish! Nah, nothing like that. Actually... I was just about to explain the W.A.L. to everyone," Bobby said.

"The wall?"

"Yeah, the Whoop-Ass Law, only one L... W.A.L."

"The Whoop-Ass Law... I like that! If this idea does become a bill--," Bobby cut Lee off, "Hold up partner! If? What do you mean if? I didn't bring the team clear across the country for no if… you mean when!"

"Right! When… it becomes a bill, I doubt they'll call it Anything like that. But I like it! Handle your business!"

"Count on it!" Bobby said.

Bobby ended the call and put his phone away. Turning back to the people, "Now, as I was saying… the time has come to introduce you people to the W.A.L. And no… I'm not talking about anything that has to do with our southern border, nor am I talking about some kind of game show. The W.A.L., that I'm speaking of, has only one L. This W.A.L. is the new and coming Whoop-Ass Law."

"Man, what the hell is this?" Frank asked.

"Glad you asked, you're about to find out!"

Bobby spoke to the crowd, "You see everyone in here right now, is trespassing. Now, Frank may have invited you here, but he doesn't have the authority to do so, because this is not really his property. Just like all the other properties he has been using, the owners have no idea about what's going on. Therefore, no consent was given for the use of the property. And with no consent being given, well, sorry to say… but that kind of makes all of you, trespassers." All of the partygoers became genuinely concerned, as they looked around at one another.

"Now, before any of you decide to make a mad dash for the door, just know that there's only one available exit, and it's currently closed." Everyone could see the three big guys with big guns, from Bobby's team, blocking the exit.

"That means you're gonna have to hear me out. So, you all are trespassing, and you all are gonna have to pay. According to the W.A.L., payment comes in part by way of punishment. Now, before you get too excited, I can tell you that, not everyone will be punished to the same extent.
Since it was Mr. Frank and his goons, who are the initiators of this event, their punishment will be to serve as an example of how the W.A.L. works. And as for the rest of you, even though you're guests, you still are trespassers, and you still must pay. But your punishment shall simply be to watch.

But I can assure you that you will not enjoy it! Hopefully, what you're about to witness, will cause you to think twice before you consciously and willfully attend events such as this, which clearly makes you all trespassers, and could land you all in jail. Also, hopefully, this will cause you to think twice before committing any other type of crime."

Bobby motioned to have Watch Boy brought up first. He stepped over to Watch Boy and addressed him by his real name. To Watch Boy's surprise, Bobby began sharing with everyone, some details of his life.

"Thomas Brown, aka Watch Boy. Honor roll at Ward Elementary. Honor roll at Jennings Middle School. 3.6 G.P.A. at Mack High. Letters of acceptance from USC, BYU, and Stanford, likely to have a very promising career. Also, I understand you were pretty good on the track. Your life was headed in a positive direction, that is..." Bobby pointed to Frank, "until you ran into this guy!"

Bobby found another one of Frank's guys to speak about. "Mr. Jackson! Your grandfather, Randall, after whom you were named, studied law at U.C.L.A. He moved to Virginia, where he practiced for many years before becoming 'Judge Randall Jackson.' Your dad, however, took a very different road. He fell in love with the bottle and drank himself to death. But you... you chose a different path. I checked you out. You also did well in school. But rather than continue in the footsteps of the good man you were named after... you chose to run with the likes of this thug!" Again, he pointed to Frank.

Bobby turned to the crowd of partygoers, "You see... I do my homework. And I'm sure you will be shocked to learn that, as for a good many of you... I know your story."

Bobby called out a few names from the crowd. "Cynthia Lions, just hired at one of the nation's most popular banks. What do you think would happen if you appeared on the evening news in connection with these guys?" He continued calling out names. "Shannon Walker, a high-ranking law student. Who knows... perhaps someday you could be chosen to defend or even prosecute, some of the very same people… that you're in here partying with… and also breaking the law with. Wow! Now wouldn't that be something?"

Bobby paced the floor a bit while looking over the crowd of partygoers. Everyone was very surprised that he knew so much about them. They were all hoping that he didn't call them out next. Bobby called out, "Carl Lee Jenkins. Of all the people in here you surprise me, or should I say… disappoint me, the most! Your father, the great Pastor Jenkins, a good man, always trying to do good for the community, would be so disappointed to learn that his only son takes part in this kind of scandalous activity. I believe it's about time now… for the first example."

Members of Bobby's team stood Watch Boy up and removed his clothing down to his briefs, "I think that many of you may be familiar with the term, 'Sparing the Rod,' and you know what it means. Back in the days of old, the rod, in most cases, was only a metaphor, for a disciplinary tool. The long and short of it is, it served to help make a child grow up to become a good respectable person. And it worked very well! Society as a whole… wasn't nearly as bad back then, as it has become in this day and age.

Somewhere along the way, some folks decided that it would be a good idea to ban the use of the rod. No more spankings in school. No more spankings in the home. They thought it better to try something like; a time out, go stand in a corner, add on a few extra chores, but only for a week or so. I'm talking about chores that they probably should have been doing anyway. There's just not enough fear and respect that comes from that type of parenting. The results are kids that grow up disrespecting their parents. Many use strong sarcasm when speaking to them. Some go as far as to curse them out, and some even physically assault their parents. In many cases, because of the bad behavior, that has been allowed to take place in the home, we now see the manifestation as it spills onto the streets of our society.

These days, young folks are disrespecting themselves and everyone around them, including law enforcement personnel. They rape, rob, and kill, without any remorse.

So, they go to prison; they play cards, play basketball, lift weights, and watch TV for a while, only to get out and become repeat offenders. No fear... No respect! I don't care what your dictionary, your teacher, or anyone else says... I say fear and respect are intertwined. They go hand and hand. So, I would just say to parents all around the world, do not spare the rod. For many, it could be an absolute deterrent from a life of crime and imprisonment. The rod could actually save your child's life!"

By now, everyone had figured out what's about to go down. Bobby continued, "So now, it's time to apply the rod, which by now, I'm sure most of you know it's just a metaphor for a good ass whipping. Though the rod was lawfully taken away many years ago... the new W.A.L. brings it back, giving power and authority back to the parent, back to the teacher, and even to law enforcement."

First up was Watch Boy. Bobby turned to Watch Boy, "You're not so bad, nor shall be your punishment." Watch Boy received a mild whipping, administered by members of Bobby's team. The partygoers mumbled among themselves as they watched. As soon as they finished with Watch Boy, "Next up... Mr. Boyd," Bobby said.
Members of Bobby's team brought Aaron Boyd out front and center. Boyd was a big strong guy. Though he struggled to resist, his efforts were to no avail, because both his hands and feet were bound. Bobby spoke to Boyd,

"So, you think you wanna be a bad ass, huh? A real big man! Part of Frank's gang of thugs! Well... here's a little taste of your reward! Compliments of Mr. Frank!"

Team members gave Aaron a good whipping. His whipping was quite a bit more severe than that which was given to Watch Boy. After a while, Aaron broke down, yelling and crying like a child. The partygoers could hardly stand to watch as they flinched with each lash that was given to Aaron. Bobby said to the partygoers, "I told you, this would not be pretty, and that you would not enjoy it. Keep in mind that under the new law, this could be any one of you, should you choose to continue running with the wrong crowd!"

He turns to Frank, who was being closely guarded by members of the team. Frank spoke out to Bobby, "You a sick ass, you know that? Man, I ain't taking no damn whipping from you, or nobody else!"

Bobby turned back to the crowd of partygoers, "He's right, Mr. Frank will not be getting a whipping... not here... and not tonight! Since his deeds are so much worse than everyone else's, likewise... shall be his punishment! Make no mistake about it, we're not sparing him... we're sparing you! You see, he and the rest of his gang will be getting theirs later. Many of you would not be able to stomach what he's gonna receive." Bobby turned back to Frank. He stared at Frank, with a look of disgust on his face, then gave an order to his team, "Get him out of my sight!" They lay hands on Frank. He struggled as he spewed out threats, "Get off me! Don't you touch me! Man get your hands off me, gotdammit! Bobby, I'll get your ass for this! You a dead man! You hear me? You a dead man! You sick ass bastard... you dead, damn-it!"

Frank was overpowered by Bobby's men. As they took him away, Bobby said, "Way to go, Mr. Frank... before all these witnesses you've just added murder threats to your long list of charges."

Bobby turned and spoke to the other two gang leaders, Double R and Big Will, "As for you two gentlemen, you should take what you've just witnessed, back to your people and let them know that the W.A.L., is coming!"

After Bobby had given warning to the other two gang leaders, he turned and addressed the crowd. "Okay everyone, the show is over. From here on, the next time you're invited to a party, you better make sure that the person doing the inviting has the authority to do so! The exit is now open. Please be careful as you leave this place."

All of the drugs were confiscated by Bobby's team and anonymously turned over to the proper authorities.

CHAPTER

22

The People's Voice
(Third Pitch - A Hit)

City officials attended the neighborhood meeting on Saturday, the seventh week following the rape and murder of Paula Gaines. Michelle gave a broad introduction of the guest panel.

"I'm sure many of you recognize the ladies and gentlemen to my right... our city officials, which include our mayor, the great Jim Hogan, which we will hear from shortly. But first, the gentleman to my left will come and share with us a very real solution to the gun control problem that plagues our nation. Ladies and gentlemen, I give you... Mr. Leander Cross!" Lee received a warm welcome, with clapping of hands, as he came forward.

After a quick handshake, Michelle took her seat. Lee addressed the crowd, "Thank you so much! Well... it's my pleasure to be here. As many of you already know, Michelle and I have been collaborating on a solution for gun control, or should I say, the lack thereof, as well as a few other types of crime that I believe we can fix. So far, we've met with city officials, heads of state, and we've even taken our concerns all the way to Washington."

The mentioning of Washington, raise the eyebrows of some of the city officials. Lee continued, "I'm proud to say that our ideas have received some positive responses." The mentioning of getting a positive response, from Washington, got the attention of the city officials, even more so, as they looked to one another, nodding their heads, indicating a genuine interest.

Continuing, Lee said, "But, as you can imagine, there was also a great deal of concern, as it should be, just as it was with some of your local officials, as to how well such measures would go over with you... THE PEOPLE."

The crowd looked around checking out the reactions of one another. They paid close attention as Lee continued to speak. He said, "You see, we're not talking about things like, holding rallies or marching in the streets, building neighborhood youth centers, or placing a bunch of peacekeeping flyers throughout the community. I'm not knocking any of those ideas. They're all good! The problem is... they're just not far reaching enough. I think those ideas, mostly reach the ones who are already good law-abiding people anyway. What I'm talking about is reaching the ones who are much more likely to engage in criminal activities. I'm talking about an absolute deterrent for such a group. I'm talking about something that will save a whole lot of lives. Not maybe... or might. Not we hope... but absolutely will." Again, the people looked around the room at one another. Everyone seemed to agree as they nodded their heads in favor of what they were hearing. Continuing, Lee said, "Now, let me just say this, before diving into the details.

These ideas will call for taking some very serious measures. Some of you may even see them as a bit invasive. But before drawing that conclusion, you should ask yourselves, are these ideas worth considering if they will save the lives of your children, your spouse, your siblings, your parents, or possibly your own? So now, if you're ready for some details, Michelle may want to come forward and render them to you at this time, after which I will return to further explain along with an interesting scenario."

Lee turned to Michelle with a hand gesture to offer her the floor. Michelle smiled, as she politely declined, "You know what... you're doing so well, why don't you just go ahead with it."

"Very well," Lee said, "Okay... So here it is... The solution is..." He spoke, as he wrote on the board, "CHIPPED DETECTION and RANDOM INSPECTIONS." He continued, "Now, I know that alone doesn't tell you a whole lot. So let me throw a few real-life situations at you... to kind of help you understand exactly what it is that I'm talking about. As I share some of the details with you, I'm Hopeful that you can see and understand how this idea could work. Also, I hope you'll appreciate just how well... it would work!"

Again, he spoke, while writing on the board, "DETECTION FOR FIREARMS." He said, "first, we... the PEOPLE and the GOVERNMENT... order all gun manufactures to chip every weapon they make. Going forward, this would include every gun, that is to be manufactured, as well as those, that have already been manufactured and distributed. Now, of course, to accomplish this, there would have to be a mandatory recall order issued to all manufacturers, as well as a mandatory response order issued to all gun owners. Notice the key word here... ALL. It doesn't matter if we're talking about, gun shops, private dealers, collectors, officers of the law, or civilians. It doesn't matter, if you possess a license to carry, or if you hold any kind of special weapons permit. ALL means ALL!

The grandfather clause would not apply here. ALL individuals who choose to own and/or carry a firearm, must possess proper identification. Notice again, the emphasis placed on the word ALL. That's because all persons found to be incompliant, will be warned and fined. If they are found to be incompliant a second time, they will be charged and dealt with as criminals." Again, he speaks while writing on the board, "DETECTION FOR DWELLINGS."

"All dwellings... and yes... there's that little big word again, ALL... commercial, residential, public, or private, must... and there's another keyword MUST... have permanent detection devices installed."

Lee asked a question of the person standing by the door in the back of the room, "Those doors are not locked, are they?" The doorman responded, "No sir, they're not." Lee said, "Good! I just wanted to make sure that our panel of authorities don't feel trapped in here. You know, just in case they start to lose their courage and decide they wanna high tail it out of here."

There was soft laughter from the crowd. Lee continued, "But I'm hoping that's not the case. I'm hoping they dare to stick around and hear me out. And I'm hoping that you will as well. So, are you with me so far?" The crowd responded, "Yes!" Lee asked, "Shall I go on?" Everyone responded favorably as some shouted, "Yeah, let's hear it!"

"Great," Lee said. Once again, he spoke as he wrote the word, "INSPECTIONS." Continuing, he said, "We would need careful vetting, when it comes to the selection of officials chosen for the task. Officials will be required to undergo comprehensive training, which shall include showing a proper level of respect, without any kind of stereotypical profiling or biased behavior, as they are ordered to conduct random inspections. Such inspections shall include all types of dwellings, all types of transportation, and even pedestrian traffic. Notice the words; RANDOM, STEREOTYPE, and BIASED. These officials could stop you at any time... not just because, you have a broken taillight, you swerved out of your lane, you are Hispanic, Black, Indian, or Asian, but, at random!

Now... not to be redundant here... but I do feel the need to reiterate just a bit. Specially selected officials! Well trained to show respect! No racial profiling! The bottom line... these officials will be fair! Otherwise, not only will they be removed, but they themselves will be dealt with firmly and quickly. Okay, I'm almost done. So, we said that the best solution for gun control is detection and inspection. So now just a quick scenario to show you how this would all work, and unless there are any questions, I'm done!" One member of the crowd said, "Take your time!" Another said, "Yeah, sound's good so far!" Lee responded, "Thank you!"

Lee offered a scenario, "So, let's say that Mr. John Doe, who happens to be a really good guy, gets up early Sunday morning, leaving his gun at home as he takes his family to church. While the family is away, thugs break into John's home, and among other items taken, they also steal his gun. But, unbeknownst to the thugs, as soon as the chipped gun travels beyond one hundred feet of the stationary base unit (SBU), authorities are instantly alerted, and the gun is now being tracked. Authorities will attempt to contact Mr. John Doe, prompting him to send the proper code. If the correct code is not received within the ample time allotted, authorities will be dispatched to confiscate the weapon and arrest the unauthorized weapon bearer.

Perhaps a good response time allotment could be something like thirty to sixty seconds, depending on location and circumstances. For instance, if a high-powered rifle is stolen and seems to be heading toward a place for large gatherings; a concert, theater, school, or church, the response time allotted, to send code, would be little to none before authorities would be dispatched.

So, the thugs have taken possession of Mr. John Doe's gun. They have beef, and a score to settle, with a guy known as Little Henry. They know that Little Henry and his girlfriend, Janice, are at the North Gate Movie Theater.

The thugs arrive at the theater with plans to shoot Little Henry. They wait in their vehicle for Henry to come out. The movie ends. A crowd of people exits the theater. The thugs spot Little Henry and his girl. Also in the crowd, exiting the theater, are three innocent children, who just happen to be in close proximity to Little Henry. The thugs get out of their car ready to launch a surprise attack. But, as soon as they step out of their vehicle, the surprise is on them, as they find themselves surrounded by the authorities who have been tracking them ever since the gun traveled one hundred feet beyond the stationary base unit (SBU).

Now I ask you... can anyone see how the gun chip could save a whole lot of lives here? Check it out... a gun was stolen. Police were alerted instantly. The gun was tracked. Among a crowd of innocent people, a shooting was planned. Authorities intervened. No lives were lost."

The crowd cheered with the clapping of hands. Lea continued, "Now, right here, right now... you're the first community, Indianapolis the first city, and, Indiana is the first state, to receive this information that could and/or should become a proposed bill."

With everyone's undivided attention, Lee continued, "Right now, you have the unique opportunity to become trailblazers by leading the way, in America's quest, for **real gun control**! You can make your voices heard, by letting your city and state officials know that you are all in favor of, this new gun control bill that could make America, a gun smart nation. One more thing... and I'll take my seat!"

Continuing, Lee said, "Suppose the three kids, that were near Little Henry, were your children. Suppose Little Henry's girlfriend was your daughter, or... suppose Little Henry was your son. Now... suppose there was, no chip, no detection, no alert, no tracking, and last but not least, no quick police intervention. You know... kind of how things are at the present."

121

Lee took a brief pause to kind of let this picture simmer in the minds of the crowd. He continued, "I know you feel that. I feel it too. All of a sudden, this picture's not looking so good, huh? Now, without gun control, just imagine how different this story might have ended.

Without gun control... far too many lives are being lost every day! With gun control... many lives would be saved... every day! So, I ask you, which will you choose? Will it be LIFE... with gun control... or... will it be DEATH... without it? Thank you!" The crowd gave Lee an ebullient round of applause as he took his seat.

Michelle returned to the podium. "Wow! That was a lot of information, huh? Certainly, an idea I believe, that is well worth considering," she said. "And now... at this time a man that needs no introduction, one that we all know and love... ladies and gentlemen, I give you our very own... Mayor Jim Hogan."

The crowd stood and applauded as the mayor came to the podium. He and Michelle shared a brief embrace, and after which, Michelle took her seat.

Turning to the crowd, the mayor shouted, "Good afternoon everyone! Please be seated. Well, let me just say, first... that I concur with Michelle's response, so much so that I kind of feel the need to reiterate just a bit. Wow! That really was, a lot of information. Very serious ideas, well worth considering, especially if they're gonna save lives. And the scenario that was given... is very much in line with the occurrences that we see or hear about in the news almost daily. But, as interesting as this all sounds... I'm sure you can imagine that these ideas come with some serious concerns. As for me... by far, the greatest of all the concerns are those of THE PEOPLE. After all, as mayor of this great city... I work for you! THE PEOPLE!

I'm here today because I need to see firsthand... just how you... THE PEOPLE... really feel about all of these new proposed gun control ideas. Are any of these ideas the kind of things that you would welcome?

Is this something you feel that you could or would, embrace? I'm certainly not here trying to shove anything down your throat. I'm just here to get your opinion.

Now, I must tell you… that to initiate and enforce something, as powerful as this, will require a great deal of effort and strategy. But I will say this, the idea does seem like a no-brainer to me. But I need to know how you feel.

Of course, there's gonna be some opposition; financial concerns, legal concerns, and a boatload of red tape. So, before I make a move to open such a huge can of worms, and make no mistake about it… huge it will be… I just need to know that you… THE PEOPLE… are with me all the way. Thank you!"

The crowd gave a big round of applause as the mayor took his seat. Michelle returned to the podium applauding along with the crowd. She shouted, "Yes! Well, I don't know about you guys, but I'm excited! I can hardly wait to get the ball rolling, or as the mayor put it, open this huge can of worms. And now, Mr. Mayor, I have just one more thing before we take a vote.

Over the past few weeks, Mr. Cross has met with members of different Mom Groups, all of whom are advocates for gun safety and, who are in favor of the ideas that have been presented to you here today. We've invited a few members here today as our distinguished guest. They're not a part of this particular community, but their stories are relevant to the cause. These ladies are esteemed members of different chapters of different advocacy groups, some of which you may be familiar with. They are nationwide organizations consisting of millions of moms that have been affected in some way by gun violence.

These three ladies have all experienced great sorrow, having been brought upon their families by way of either the mishandling of guns or by some deliberate act of violence with a gun.

So, ladies, if you would… please stand and give us a wave as I call you names. I won't ask you to say or do anything.

I would just like to let everyone see who you are.

"**First**, we have Brenda Smith." Brenda stood and waved. Michelle continues, "Brenda's youngest sister, Margie, now deceased, lost her two-year old son, due to the mishandling of a gun. Another sister, Rose Mary, also deceased, lost her only son, also due to the mishandling of a gun. And if that wasn't enough, Brenda's very own son received thirteen bullet wounds as he drove his vehicle along the streets of Fort Wayne. Today she's thankful that God saw fit to spare his life.

Next, we have Elizabeth Giles." Elizabeth stood and waved. Michelle continued, "Liz lost both, her brother and sister-in-law, to gun violence at the hands of their very own son.

And last, but certainly not least, we have Mary J Flowers." Mary stood and waved. Michelle continued, "During the same incident, Mary lost both, her mother, and her baby sister, due to gun violence at the hands of the sister's boyfriend who later turned the gun on himself.

As I said before, I'm not asking them to speak, but they said it would be okay for me to share some of their stories. Thank you, ladies. You may be seated."

The three ladies took their seats. Michelle continued, "The message, that they wanted me to convey to you on this day is… together we stand, with chapters across the nation, tens of millions strong. And together we must continue our efforts to make not only the great city of Indianapolis… but America as a whole… a gun smart nation!

So now, by a show of hands, let me see those of you who would be in favor of and willing to support these ideas. Who wants to save lives?" Hands went up all across the room. She responded, "Very good! Now, by a show of hands, who would be opposed to these ideas?" Not a single hand went up.

"Great! Looks like we're one hundred percent in favor." The crowd applauded. Turning to the mayor, "Well, Mr. Mayor… I believe I speak for THE PEOPLE when I say… let's open that can of worms! We are with you, all the way!" There was a standing ovation. As the crowd settled down, Michelle continued, "At this time, I'd like to thank everyone for coming out and supporting such a worthy cause. Please watch your email for updates. In the meantime, if you have any questions or concerns, you have my info, please feel free to contact me. Again, thanks for coming, and have a wonderful day. We are adjourned!"

Most of the crowd dispersed rather quickly, though a few hung around and mingled for a while. Lee told Michelle that he would like to stick around for just a few minutes to have a quick one-on-one with the mayor.

"Alright," Michelle said, "Well, I'm just gonna head on home. Here's the key to this place. If you would, be so kind as to lock up, you can just bring it to me when you're done."

Michelle left and headed home. Lee went over for a quick chat with the mayor. "Well, Mr. Mayor, I can't tell you how much I appreciate you being on board with what we're trying to accomplish."

"Any such plan as significant as this, that would stand to save lives all across America, I'm happy to be a part! And with the city of Indianapolis leading the way, you bet… I'm all in," the mayor said.

"Wonderful! But you know… so far… we've only talked about part one which just deals with prevention. You see… detection and inspection, are both parts of prevention. Although part one will prevent a lot of crime from happening. There is also a part two, however… which deals with a response. This part suggest how we might respond to certain crimes if or when they may occur."

"I see! Part two, huh?"

"Yeah, so at your convenience of course… I'd like to set up a time that you and I could meet and discuss part two."

"Absolutely! Contact my office," the mayor said, "I'm sure it'll be quite interesting, to say the least.

CHAPTER

23

The Abduction

After voting, everyone had left the neighborhood center. Lee secured the building and head out to his car. As he opened the door to get in the car, Bobby called. Lee answered, "Hey Bobby!" Bobby asked, "How was the meeting, did it go well?" "Yeah, absolutely, the meeting went very well. Everyone seemed to be in favor of our ideas," Lee replied.

While standing outside of his car with the driver side door open, another car came speeding down the street. Lee took notice as the driver intentionally swerved toward him. With quick thinking, he leaped onto the hood of his car, rolled over and off the passenger side.

The speeding driver knocked the door completely off Lee's car. Even without a driver's side door, Lee hopped into his car and gave chase.

There was heavy traffic on the main streets. The speeding driver darted in and out of traffic and ran through red lights. Lee hoped to get close enough to get a license plate number but, as the driver nearly hit a young mother pushing her baby in a stroller, Lee decided to back off. The speeding driver got away.

Michelle arrived home. As normal, she pulled into the garage and lowered the door. She got out of the car and went inside. Upon entering her home, the kitchen usually was her first stop, and it was no different this time. She sat her purse on the bar and checked her phone for missed calls. Soon after checking her phone, she headed to her bedroom with intent to slip into something more comfortable.

As soon as Michelle stepped through the doorway to her bedroom, she got surprised by three guys who were hiding and waiting for her to come in. Michelle, being a former self-defense instructor, and current fitness enthusiast, was able to fight them off just enough to make a break for it. She ran into the living room, hoping to get out of the front door. Two of the guys who chased her were close on her tail. There was not enough time to get out of the door, after barely getting it open. There were two ways to enter the living room, which were from the foyer, and from the kitchen. Michelle decided to make a break for the kitchen, but she got cut off by the third guy.

The three guys now had her trapped in the living room. She put up quite a struggle, making a total mess of the room until one of the guys put a chloroform rag over her nose rendering her unconscious. They took her into the garage and loaded her into the back seat of her car. They had her bound and lying flat so that the neighbors would not see anything that would look suspicious as they pulled out of the garage. They lowered the garage door, leaving everything from outside of the home looking normal, as they drove away.

The three guys took Michelle to Big Will's place. Big Will was there and waiting for Michelle's arrival. The three guys tossed her onto a sofa as Big Will began to make threats against Michelle, her daughter, and Lee.

"I know all about your little neighborhood meetings. I've heard about your ideas and plans to go up against hard-working people like my man Frank, Double R, and myself. Do you really think we are just going to sit back and watch you guys mess up what we got going, huh? Ain't gonna happen! I don't give a damn, if it's you, your partner, or the damn mayor... you start messing with my money... people are going to get hurt! So, for your own good... I'm gonna need you to go to your next meeting and tell the people that you've had a change of heart. Tell them that you think it's best to leave things as they are. Tell them that you're canceling your quest for gun control. And if they know what's good for them... they'll do the same! I've seen this Bobby guy... and members of his team. I know they're probably gonna come around here looking for you. And you can bet on this... my guys will be ready to greet them when they arrive. But you won't be here. I'm taking you someplace out of the way until I'm done dealing with them."

Lee went to Michelle's house to return the key. He rang the doorbell several times, but there was no answer. As he knocked on the door, it swung slightly open. Slowly, He entered the house. With an ominous feeling, he called out her name. As he looked around, he could clearly see signs of a struggle.

Lee thought to check the garage. Michelle's car was gone. Deciding to try and contact her, he reached for his cell phone, before realizing that he must have dropped it back at the neighborhood center, during the incident with the speeding driver. Using Michelle's house phone, Lee made a call to her cell. The cell phone rang, but he discovered that it was actually in the kitchen lying on the bar. He knew that Michelle would never go anywhere leaving her cell phone behind. He believed that he knew exactly what had happened.

Lee returned to the center and found his cell phone lying near the curb. He grabbed the phone and called Bobby. Quickly answering his phone, Bobby asked, "Hey man, what happened? We seem to have got cut off. I tried calling you back several times, but no answer. What's going on?"

"We got a problem! They tried to take me out. And they've got Michelle!" Lee said.

"Son of a… well, I know I probably don't have to ask, But, just to dot my I's and cross my T's… you didn't call the cops, did you?"

"Hell no! Are you kidding me? I want her back today! You and I both know… if we involve the cops, it could be weeks before we know anything!"

CHAPTER 24

Search and Rescue

Lee and Bobby met to try and figure out who was behind it all. Bobby told Lee that both, Double R and Big Will, were present at Frank's warehouse party. He also mentioned that they were both leaders of their own gangs, and they seemed to be closely associated with Frank and his gang of thugs. They figured that since Frank and his gang have been taken down, the hit attempt and the abduction had to be the workings of; Double R, Big Will, or both.

Lee, Bobby, and members of the team, hit several popular clubs and hangouts seeking info on Double R and Big Will. After hitting several spots, they finally gained info on Double R, but nothing on Big Will.

The team swooped down on Double R's gang, and shook them up pretty well, only to find out that they were completely innocent. They were not even aware of Michelle's abduction. Lee and Bobby figure it had to be the work of Big Will and his gang.

The team split up as they hit a few more clubs, seeking info on Big Will. No one seemed to know or have any useful info on Big Will, or if they did, they were afraid to talk.

After coming up empty on info about Big Will, they decide to put pressure on Frank to make him roll on Big Will. It worked. Frank broke under pressure and told them everything they wanted to know. The team collaborated, and devised a strategy, to bring down Big Will and his gang.

Big Will figured that Lee, Bobby, and the team would come looking to rescue Michelle. He knew that his hangout would probably be one of the first places they hit. He ordered a few of his guys to be there and ready to entertain Bobby's team when they arrived. Big Will and some of his other guys had taken Michelle and were held up in a suite at the Hotel Royale.

The bad guys were able to get Michelle to cooperate by lying to her, saying that they had Lindsey, and if she ever wanted to see her daughter alive again, she'd better cooperate, if not, the next time she saw her daughter, she would be lying in a box. The fear of harm possibly being done to her daughter was enough to get Michelle to walk calmly through the lobby, without alarming the staff in any kind of way. She entered the elevator, and on to the room where they would continue to hold her hostage.

While Lee, Bobby and some of the team members were still checking out different clubs around town, a few other members of Bobby's team, arrived at Big Will's hang out. One of Big Will's guys called to inform him that the opposition had arrived. On the phone, Big Will responded, "Good! Give them a nice little welcome party!"

At Big Will's hangout, shots rang out all over the place. Bobby's team were all sharpshooters. They were able to take Big Will's guys down without killing them.

They forced the guys to talk, spilling the beans on Big Will and Michelle's whereabouts.

Team members relayed the info, on Will's location, to Lee, Bobby, and the others. The team arrived at the Hotel Royale. Lee and Bobby approached the manager at the front desk to inquire about the room number for Willie Green (Big Will). The manager was reluctant to give out any information on their guests as it was against hotel policy. Discreetly, and in a very serious manner, they told the manager that they have reason to believe that a female is being held hostage in the hotel. The manager was still hesitant, to give out information on Will. He was a bit startled when Lee stepped behind the counter, and told him, "We've positioned a whole team in and around this place. Now, we can do this one of two ways... We can rescue the lady in a very quiet and discreet manner, or we can make a whole lot of noise upsetting all of your guests and putting your hotel all over the evening news. Either way, we're getting her out of here!"

The warning from Lee, was enough to persuade the manager, to give up the info on Big Will and his party, and to hand over the keys to the suite. Lee relayed the info to the rest of the team that were present.

Big Will and a few of his guys were down at the bar having drinks and flirting with some of the servers. Dale and Trevor were left in the suite to watch over Michelle.

Dale decided, he was going to have a little fun his way. He told Trevor to stand guard, just outside of the door, and to alert him if someone was coming. Dale went into the bedroom area of the suite where Michelle was restrained. She could tell by his demeanor, that he was about to try something, and she knew exactly what was on his mind. Duct tape covered her mouth. Both her hands and feet were zip-tied and taped. She sat in a chair completely helpless. Slowly Dale started, circling around Michelle, making her very uncomfortable. Suddenly, he picked her up out of the chair and flung her onto the bed.

Brittany, a member of Bobby's team, who appeared as

a little old lady, dressed in a housekeeping uniform, came to enter the room directly across the hall from Big Will's suite where Trevor was standing guard at the door. "Will you be needing room service or fresh towels or anything?" Brittany asked.

"No thanks, we're good," Trevor responded.

"Well, alright, just holler if you need anything," she said.

Brittany opened the door and went into the suite across the hall, leaving the cart in the doorway. She proceeded to the bathroom where she texted Donna, another member of Bobby's team. Moments later, Donna came out of a room that was two doors down from where Trevor was standing. Donna was dressed in a very skimpy two-piece swimsuit. She walked right by Trevor. In passing, she smiled and spoke as she appeared to be on her way to the elevator to head down to the pool. As she got near the corner where she would turn toward the elevators, she dropped a bag, of which the contents spilled onto the floor. She then dropped her towel as she slowly bent over to pick up her belongings. Trevor got an eye full as she gathered up everything except a case for her contact lenses. After gathering her belongings, she disappeared around the corner, heading for the elevators.

Trevor saw that Brittany had left her contact case lying on the floor. Being duped into responding like a gentleman, Trevor went with the intent to retrieve the contact case and return it to Brittany. He grabbed the case and as soon as he turned the corner, he was met by two, male members of Bobby's team, one of which knocked him out cold. They took him to the room, that Donna had come out of, and tied him up.

By now, Dale had gotten his shirt off, Michelle's blouse opened, and her pants unfastened. "Yeah, pretty lady, you know what time it is. We bout to have ourselves a little party, you know... pick it up where your little friend left off," Dale said.

Brittany, from across the hall still dressed as a little old lady housekeeper, used her key card to enter the suite.

Dale could hear her as she entered. He shouted from the bedroom to the person entering the sitting area of the suite, who he thought was Trevor, "Yo man... is someone coming? If not I'm gonna need you to hang out there for a minute. I'm kind of busy in here right now, dawg!"

"Oh, don't mind me, just housekeeping, bringing you some fresh towels," Brittany responded.

Realizing that it was not Trevor, who had just entered the room, Dale jumped up. "What? Fresh towels? Housekeeping?" He was about to head into the sitting area when Brittany, with an arm full of towels, met him in the doorway of the bedroom.

"How did you get in here, and where the hell is Trevor?" Dale asked.

"You mean the young man outside the door? He just stepped away to the snack machine. So where would you like for me to leave the towels?" Brittany asked.

Dale knocked all the towels out of Brittany's hand, "We don't need no damn towels, old lady... just get the hell out of here!" He shoved Brittany backward. She fell against the bed. Helpless, Michelle could only watch as she feared for Brittany, who she thought was just a sweet little old lady trying to do her job.

Dale made an advanced toward Brittany. She sprung up with a kick to his midsection followed by a quick jab to the throat. While gagging and gasping for air, he took a swing at her. Being a well-trained fighter, Brittany ducked, grabbed his arm and popped his elbow out of the socket, before body-slamming him to the floor. She continued to give Dale a pretty good beating.

Michelle was amazed by what she was seeing. Two of Bobby's team members rushed in to restrain Dale. Brittany took out a blade, cut the zip ties, and removed the tape to free Michelle. Michelle realized that this was not just some sweet little old lady. She also figured out that these people, who had come to her rescue, must be members of Lee and Bobby's team.

Brittany led Michelle out and down to the lobby.

She pointed to a car that was staged for their getaway, "You see the little red mustang there… the keys are in it. Go ahead, start it up, and be ready to drive, I'll be right out," Brittany said. She went to the manager and suggested that he have his bar employees discretely ask their innocent patrons to leave calmly, so as not to alarm the bad guys. As the employees carried out their instructions, Jeff, Will's right-hand man, started to notice as people in the bar were being whispered to in their ear, and soon after, they got up to ease out. He sensed that something was up.

Michelle passed the bar on her way out. Big Will's back was turned, but Jeff spotted her as she was heading for the car.

"Hey! The bitch is getting away!" He said.

Big Will turned around and saw her, "What the hell… get her!" He shouts. The guys got up to give chase, but before getting out of the bar area, they were confronted by members of Bobby's team. The confrontation resulted in an outbreak of fighting and gunfire. People panicked and started running and screaming. "So much for being discrete and avoiding the evening news," The manager said to himself.

Michelle made it to the car. She was soon joined by Brittany and Donna. Big Will and his right-hand man, Jeff, broke away from the action to give chase after the ladies as they sped off. Lee and Bobby also broke away from the action to go after Will and Jeff. Being incredibly good at doing so, the rest of Bobby's team disappeared as soon as the police arrived. The police captured Will's guys and confiscated all of their weapons. They later confirmed that the guns, which were taken from the hotel, as well as the ones that were confiscated from Big Will's clubhouse, were all stolen.

Three cars raced through the streets, causing near misses and crashes here and there. Big Will was hot on Michelle's tail, and Lee was hot on his.

Jeff hung out of the passenger side of Will's car, shooting at the ladies. The ladies ducked and weaved as they continued to speed away. The ladies zipped through a busy intersection. Looking in his rearview mirror, Big Will got distracted when he noticed Lee and Bobby on his tail. As he went through the intersection, he saw a very big truck, with a very loud horn, coming right at them. In an attempt to avoid the truck, he swerved, causing him to lose control of his vehicle and crash into a business. Lee and Bobby pulled up just as Jeff was getting out of the car. Right away, Jeff started shooting at them. Jeff and Bobby exchanged several rounds before Bobby put him down.

Big Will got out of his car to face Lee, who had a gun drawn on him.

"So, what's it gonna be old school... you gonna shoot an unarmed man, or what?" Big Will asked.
Laying his gun on the hood of his car, Lee said, "No, I'm not gonna shoot you... I'd get no pleasure from that. I'm just gonna kick your ass real good!"

"Bring it on, old man. First, I'll take care of your ass, then I'll go after that bitch!" The two men engaged in a very physical confrontation. As a younger guy, big, strong, and solid, Will got the early upper hand. Lee possessed a technique that would outweigh physical size and strength. Bobby watched closely with his gun in hand, ready to intervene if necessary. But he kind of knew that an intervention would probably not be necessary as he was fully aware of the fact that, Lee was a person who happens to be a highly skilled fighter.

When the fight was over, Lee stood in victory, and Big Will was out cold.

"Bravo! I see you still got it," Bobby said to Lee.

"Yeah, well, you could have just shot him and ended this thing a whole lot sooner, you know," Lee responded.

"Now why would I do that... and rob you of all your glory? Besides... that would go against all we're trying to accomplish. We're fighting for gun control, remember... not for a chance to shoot up people."

Lee looked at Bobby, then at Jeff, as he lay wounded on the ground, and then back at Bobby.

"Well, now... that's different," Bobby said, "he was shooting at me. So... I had to put him down!"

CHAPTER

25

GUNMEN AT THE RESTAURANT

A few days after being rescued from her abductors, Michelle sat in a booth opposite Lee at one of her favorite seafood restaurants. A little time was spent looking over the menu. After deciding on a selection, Lee folded his menu and laid it down on the table.

"Well," Lee said, "I think I know what I'll have. So, you just take your time, while I run to the restroom, and I'll be right back."

Soon after Lee entered the restroom, a guy with a handgun entered the restaurant. The gunman approached an employee at the cash register. He pointed the gun to the employee's head. People nearby were shocked and frightened.

The gunman shouted at the employee, "Open that register!" The employee was also shocked and frozen in fear. The gunman continued, "Now, dammit! Hurry up!"

In the restroom, with the noisy sounds of toilets flushing, urinals flushing, hand dryers blowing, water running, washing of hands, and paper towel dispensers, Lee was oblivious to the situation unfolding just outside in the foyer.

The employee tried frantically to open the register, but he couldn't get it to open.

"Come on," the gunman shouted," stop stalling dammit! Hurry up!"

"I just came on duty, it won't open for me because I have not been signed on to this register yet," The employee said.

"Well, sign on dammit!" The gunman said.

"I can't do anything, I'm locked out. The manager has to enter a code before anyone can sign on."

"Where is your manager," asked the gunman?

"Probably in his office," the employee responded.
The gunman puts his gun very close to the employee's face, "Well, get his ass out here!"

"Alright, alright!"
The employee made the call for the manager over the intercom, "I need a manager to register one please, manager to register one. Emergency!"

Still in the restroom, while washing his hands, Lee noticed the emergency call over the intercom, but quickly dismissed it.

Out in the foyer, with the gun pointed right at the employee's face, the gunman shouted, "Hey! What the hell are you doing? You trying to be slick, huh? You trying to send some kind of signal or something, huh? Don't mess with me man! I'll blast your ass right now! you hear me?"

"Yes, alright, okay, no signal," the employee said.
The gunman shouted, "On the floor! Now!"
The employee complied as he Kneeled down to the floor, "Alright!"

"Lie down!" The gunman shouted.

The employee begged, "Please don't shoot!"

"Shut up! Don't you move a muscle... or I'll blast your ass... you got that?" Nearly scared to death, the employee responded, "Yeah, okay."

The manager arrived on the scene. Coming in from behind the gunman, the manager couldn't see the gun and therefore he had no clue as to what was taking place. As the manager got closer, he saw his employee on the floor and started to rush to his aid. The gunman turned to the manager. The manager received an unpleasant greeting by way of the perpetrator's gun being stuck in his face. He was startled for a moment, but quickly realized what was going down. The gunman asked, "Are you the manager?"

"Yes, I am," The manager replied.

"Good! Now get that freaking register open, right now, or I'm gonna start shooting people... starting with you!"

Lee came out of the restroom and quickly realize what was taking place. He heard the manager say to the gunman, while opening the register, "Okay, take what you want, please... just take what you want and go. No need to hurt anyone." The gunman shouted at the manager, "Shut-up, I'll do the talking here! Just handover the damn money, and no one has to get hurt!"

Lee decided to sneak up on the gunman from behind. He got close enough to intervene. Lee said to the gunman, "Excuse me, sir!"

"What!" The gunman shouted as he made a hostile turn toward Lee, intending to stick his gun in Lee's face, "Can't you see we kind of biz--" His speech got cut off as Lee grabbed the gun with one hand and jabbed the gunman in the face with the other. The gun went off, firing rapid rounds into the ceiling until it was empty. The people that were gathered around, all hit the floor. No one was hit. With a second punch to the face, the gunman hit the floor in a daze. Lee got the gun away from the gunman and handed it to the manager, "Here, you'd better hang on to this." Lee took his belt off and began whipping and lecturing the gunman, "So, you wanna be a bad ass, huh?

You think you can just go around robbing folks? Think you can Just go taking shit that doesn't belong to you? You think you're something special... too good to work? Maybe, you're just too damn lazy to get a job. Well, whatever your deal is... here's a little lesson that your momma and daddy should have taught you a long time ago." Between lashes, Lee shouted, "Respect... other... people's... property!"

The bystanders were all shocked. Never have they seen anything like this before. A grown man getting an old school chastising in public for committing a crime. All the bystanders were in favor of the chastising. In fact, as a showing of solidarity, most, cheered it on, while a few, both male and female, even took off their belts and got in on the action by offering a few lashes to the gunman.

At the emergency call center, an operator answered a call about a disturbance at the restaurant, "9 1 1, what's your emergency? Uh-huh, uh-huh, okay, got it!" She dispatched officers to the scene.

"All units in the area, of Top Chef Seafood, report to the scene we have a ten sixty-five in progress. Repeat... ten sixty-five in progress at Top Chef Seafood, located at 9501 E. Fairway Boulevard. Nearby units report!"

Back at the restaurant, Lee continued to whip and lecture the gunman, "You got that? Huh? The gunman responded crying, "Yeah, yeah!"
Lee repeated, "You got it?"
The gunman cried, "Yeah! Yeah man! Yeah!"
 Still beating the gunman, Lee said, "You sure you got it... or do you want me to beat your ass some more?"
The gunman cried, "Yeah! Yeah!"

"Yeah?" Lee asked, "So, you do want more?"

"No, man! Nall," the gunman said, "what's wrong with you? You crazy, man!"

"Yeah," Lee said, "just crazy enough to beat your ass! Now stay down, and don't you move!"

Police units piled into the parking lot of the restaurant. A few officers went in while others took cover on the outside. Officers entered and found the gunman lying on the floor.

The restaurant manager spoke to the officers, "I'm the manager here." He Pointed to the gunman, "This guy was trying to rob us." Handing the gun to one of the officers, "Here's his gun." The lead officer asked, "Why is he lying on the floor?"

"He's afraid of getting his ass whipped if he moves," Lee replied. Smiling and nodding his head, the lead officer said, "Sounds like the W.A.L. in action."

"You know about that?" Lee asked.

"I've heard some of the buzz," the officer said, "and I'm all for it! This here is a bit of proof that it works!" Two other cops apprehended the gunman.

"Come on! On your feet! Time to take a little ride, downtown." The gunman got up saying, "Good! Get me the hell out of here!" Referring to Lee, "that dude's crazy!"

Michelle, like Lee, had gone to the restroom herself, and with all the noise in the restroom, had missed out on all of the action. She came out just in time to see the police take the gunman away in handcuffs. She spotted Lee among the crowd and went to question him, "What's going on?" She asked.

"Oh, just some crazy guy trying to rob the place."

"Wow! Well, good thing the cops got here in time to stop him."

Lee smiled, "Yeah, right!"

The manager took to the intercom, "May I have your attention, please. This is the restaurant manager speaking. I'd like to apologize for the disturbance that we've all just had to endure. The police have apprehended the perpetrator and taken him into custody. I'm happy to say that no one was hurt, and everything is fine now. Also, I'd like to extend to all of our patrons, that are currently present, a ten percent discount off of your total bill tonight, as well as an additional twenty-five percent off of your next visit. Thank you so much for your patience. Please enjoy the rest of your evening and we hope to see you back real soon."

As with all the other customers, Lee and Michelle went on to enjoy their dining experience.

Before leaving the restaurant, Lee received a call from Bobby, letting him know that, for the most part, their business has been completed. He told Lee that most of the team will be leaving soon, except for the few who will stick around for a while to encourage Frank to do the right thing.

Lee shared with Michelle, the news about the guys leaving, "Well, it may interest you to know that Frank's gang has been completely dismantled, and a very strong message has gone out to all the others. Bobby and the team will be leaving soon, but in the coming months… I believe you're gonna see a huge reduction in crime, throughout the city of Indianapolis, especially those that are gun-related."

"Well, I certainly hope so," Michelle said, "And maybe our police can handle things from here."

"Yeah, let's hope so!"

Lee told Michelle about the next meeting with the mayor. "Also, I wanted to let you know that, before leaving the last meeting, this past Saturday, I spoke with the mayor briefly about scheduling a follow-up meeting to discuss, part two of, our gun control proposal. He told me to contact his office, I did… and that meeting is now scheduled, to take place on Monday… three weeks from today. Meanwhile, I'll be heading back to California to take care of some business. Hopefully, by the time I return, my realtor will have found a buyer."

"Well, I'm sure it will all work out," Michelle said.

On the next day, Lee boarded a flight back to California.

CHAPTER

26

Lindsey Returns Home

Lindsey returned home from her college tour. She had no idea about the situation that took place at the campsite, in her cabin, and in her bed. She never knew that Frank and his gang had made plans for her abduction, nor was she ever made aware of the circumstances that her mom had just gone through. Lindsey and her mom were overjoyed to see one another. Considering all that had happened, coupled with the possibility of all that could have gone wrong, Michelle embraced her daughter so strongly, and long, that it was a little concerning to Lindsey, who asked, "Mom, are you okay? It's only been a few days! Are you sure you're going to be okay with me going off to school?"

"Yes, dear. It's just that this is the first time that you've been away, and I've missed you so much! I'm just glad to have you home. So, tell me... how was it? I wanna hear all about it."

"Okay, but first, I need to use the restroom!"
She went to, and returned from, the restroom.

"Wow! Now that's better! I've been holding that iced coffee for a long time." She shared her experience saying,

"Okay, so, on the first day as I'm arriving to sign in, the very first person I see, as I enter the line right behind her, was none other than Tiffany. We were both so excited to see one another, that we may have created a bit of a scene by laughing, screaming, and hugging.

Soon after we both got signed in, and was heading to the next stop, we met Gena and Barb as they were arriving. So, naturally... we wait for them and together we go to meet our tour guide, Miss Angela Larson, who we often referred to as, 'Miss Ann'. She was really cool!

After being shown all around the campus, it wasn't long before we were all thinking the same thing, which was... 'this is the place for us!' When asked what we thought of the place, of course, we all said the same thing... 'we love it!' Miss Ann went on to inform us that this year, for the first time, and on a trial basis, they've added a camping trip to the tour. She took us to get our cabin assignments, which were set up for two students to a cabin. Tiffany and I shared a cabin and Gena and Barb shared one. We were hoping for neighboring cabins, but that didn't work out. Their cabin was about four or five, down the way from ours. But we still had a lot of fun. Of course, we did the usual... hot dog and marshmallow thing, you know? I mean, what's a campfire without that, right? Also in attendance were students that I knew from other schools. Each night we would alternate hosting board games in some of our cabins. One night while we were at Gena's cabin, the game lasted so long that some of the girls just stayed there and slept on the floor. I certainly didn't mind staying late that night because I was the ultimate winner and was crowned, Game Queen."

"Wow! I guess you did have a good time. So, you say this was all on a trial basis, huh?"

"Yep!"

"So, no problems of any kind?" Michelle asked.

"Nope! Not a one! Word is… they plan to continue having the camping trip as a regular part of the tour."

"Well, I'm glad you liked it, glad you all had fun, glad you all were safe, and so glad to have you back home, safe and sound."

"I'm glad to be home too, mom! But why wouldn't we be safe?"

"Well, dear, in this day and age, you just never know what could happen."

The TV Bandit

About eight weeks had passed since Paula's murder. A select group of officers had been trained and given clearance to start enforcing the new Whoop-Ass Law.

A guy had been casing a home in a nice neighborhood ever since he'd noticed a large box that was set out by the trash, that once housed a high-end, big screen TV. For several days he watched the coming and going of the people who lived there.

Finally, the bandit had figured out the schedules of the people who lived at the residence that he'd planned to hit. He now knew exactly when and how long the residence would be empty.

Early Wednesday morning, after everyone had gone, the bandit walked up to the door and rang the bell just as an extra precaution to make sure that no one was present inside of the home. After a few minutes, and a few rings of the doorbell, he decided that it was time to break in. He took a roll of boxing tape from his pocket. On a small section of the glass side panel of the front entrance, he applied the tape to prevent the glass from shattering and making what would likely be a sound that would alert the neighbors.

He punched the glass out with his fist. The alarm went off. He reached through the hole, unlocked the door from the inside and went in. Once inside, he quickly spotted the TV. He hurried to disconnect the cords and cables. He grabbed the TV and head for the door. Being that the bandit was somewhat of a small build, he found it a bit of a struggle to carry the large TV. He made his exit rather slowly, leaving the front door wide open. Before he could even make it off the property, he was greeted by two gun yielding police officers. The first officer yelled out, "Stop right there! Set the TV down, easy!" The bandit stopped and set the TV down as instructed.

"Hands in the air," the officer said, "Turn around!" The bandit had the good sense to comply with all the officer's commands. The second officer said, while putting the bandit in handcuffs, "Just cooperate and this will all go a whole lot better for you!"

The first Officer said to the bandit, "Here's what's gonna happen. We're gonna get some information from you, get a set of prints, and run a background check. Depending on what turns up, we may not have to arrest you, alright?"

"Yes sir," the bandit said. He could hardly believe, what his ears had heard, that he might get off without an arrest.

"Just have a seat right here on the lawn," said the first officer, "and I'll be right back." The second officer assisted the bandit to sit down on the ground.

The first officer ran the background check and returned. "Well, it looks like this is your lucky day. Since you have no priors, we're not going to arrest you this time. Instead, you'll be getting a warning today… a very strong warning! Have you heard about the W.A.L.?"

"Well, yeah, I've heard a little bit about… Oh hell nawl! Wait a minute now!" The bandit started to squirm as if he wanted to get up and flee the scene. "No need to go there! You ain't gotta be doing all that, now!"

The first officer pulled the W.A.L. strap from its holster, "So here it is! Your warning! First, we gonna beat that ass! Then, you gonna take the TV and put it back where you found it!

And then, you gonna take your ass home and think about what you wanna do with the rest of your life!"

"Okay-okay," the Bandit said, "I got it! You ain't gotta be doing no beating though, man! I'll just take the TV back and be on my way, man! You ain't gotta be beating on nobody. It don't take all that, man!"

"Oh, but it does! I gotta give you your warning! And if we meet again... I will arrest you and you'll be getting this treatment twice a week for every week that you spend in lockup," the first officer said.

The officer gave a strong lecture while simultaneously administering the W.A.L., to the bandit.

"Now let this be a lesson to you. You can't go around taking shit that doesn't belong to you. People work hard for the things they have. You want a big screen TV, get a job... take your ass to work like everyone else!" The bandit squirmed and cried, "Okay-okay man, okay!" Still whipping the bandit, "Now get your ass up and go put the TV back where you got it from," the first officer said.
The bandit cried, "Okay-okay!"

The two officers helped the bandit to his feet. The second officer removed the cuffs.

"Be careful with the TV," the first officer said, "you better not drop it!" The second officer escorted the bandit back inside. The bandit carefully placed the TV back in its original position and reconnected the cords and cables. The second officer escorted the bandit back outside.

"Now take your ass home," the first officer said, "and don't let me catch you back out here again! You hear me?" The officer gave the bandit one last lash, as he high tailed it out of there.

A few bystanders applauded the actions of the police.

"Do you think we did the right thing by letting him go?" the second officer asked.

"We didn't just let him go," the first officer responded, "A real good ass whipping never lets you go! I think that for most... it serves as a really good attitude adjustment. It could change one's way of thinking, so as, to possibly turn their life around.

A good ass whipping could get them headed in a more positive direction!"

As they all stood there, watching the bandit haul-ass away from the scene, the first officer continued, "Nope... we didn't just let him go, instead... I think we may have just turned him around. Yep... I think he'll be making better decisions from here on!"

CHAPTER
27

RUDE AND INDECENT

About midday Wednesday, there was normal traffic moving through the streets of Indy. Suddenly, along came an airhead driving very aggressively. He darted in and out of traffic cutting people off, causing many of them to brake and swerve out of their lanes. One of the vehicles that the airhead cut off just happened to be an unmarked police car with two on duty officers inside. The officers pulled the airhead over, and after ticketing the guy, they introduced him to the W.A.L. People passing by showed their approval as they toot their horns and shouted, "Yeah, that's right... beat that ass! Out here driving like a damn maniac!"

Parking Lot Confrontation

A lady came out of the grocery store pushing a cart with a few small bags and a gallon of milk. Before going to her car, she pushed the cart into the return corral. She took her items out from the cart and started to head toward her vehicle.

Another young lady in a convertible, came through the lot rolling about twenty-five miles per hour, which she felt was slow enough, but it was still about ten miles per hour over the posted speed limit. With the many rows of vehicles present, the two ladies didn't see one another until the one, with the groceries, had stepped well out into the aisle. At the last minute, the driver of the convertible took notice and slammed on her brakes. The lady with the groceries was frightened so much that, in a panic, she dropped her bags. Many of her items were ruined. A very heated, verbal confrontation evolved. A crowd formed as the two ladies went at it.

A police officer, who had just pulled into the lot, was going to do her own shopping when she noticed the commotion and stepped in to resolve the situation. The officer spoke to the young driver about the W.A.L. and suggested that from now on she exercise a little more caution when driving through a parking lot. She wrote the young lady a warning ticket, before sending her on her way.

Loud Music

Thursday afternoon, a senior couple sat at a red light, in the left turn lane at a major intersection. All was calm, while they waited patiently for the green light. Suddenly, a guy pulled up in the middle lane, blasting his loud obnoxious music. He had so much bass, that it not only rattled the windows and doors of his own vehicle, but it rattled the glass in the senior's car as well. The senior couple was obviously bothered by the noise.

The rude guy could see that the people were uncomfortable with his music, but he didn't care. He was inconsiderate to everyone as he continued to blast his music. A cop car, with the W.A.L. symbol on the door, pulled up in the right lane. The cop looked at the guy. The guy looked at the cop. The guy noticed the W.A.L. symbol on the door. The guy turned the music down... waaay down. The light turned green. The senior couple made their left turn. The cop turned right. The guy with the music went straight ahead, keeping his music at a moderate level.

High School Pick Up

Later in the day, a guy pulled into the parking lot of a high school to pick up his sister and a few of her girlfriends. The guy was blasting very loud music with a lot of profanity. He pulled into the student pickup lane which was less than one hundred feet from the nearest classroom. It was almost time for school to let out, but a few students were still trying to complete their tests. The students were disturbed by the loud music. The teacher felt, that if a guy had the audacity to do something like that, it was probably not a good idea to confront him.

The teacher took her concerns to the principal's office where the police were called to handle the situation. As soon as school was let out, the girls piled into the car with the guy and the loud music. Before they could get off of the lot, they found themselves surrounded by police. The police officers informed the driver, about common law nuisance, and gave him two warnings. The first was written, and the second was a physical administration of the W.A.L.

Indecent Exposure (sagging)

Friday afternoon at the Fairway Shopping Mall, two officers sitting in a cruiser, noticed a group of guys walking through the parking lot.

All of the guys were sagging but one in particular, had his pants and shorts pulled down so far that more than half of his intergluteal cleft was exposed. His appearance was very indecent, offensive, and unacceptable. The cops stopped the group and introduced the one guy to the W.A.L. The others quickly fixed their clothes to appear decent. After a good lesson, the one, also fixed his clothes and they were all sent on their way.

Indecent Exposure (thongs)

Two young ladies in their early twenties, shopping in a clothing store, were dressed rather provocatively. A middle-aged mother with two kids, approximately seven and eight years old, was also shopping in the same section of the store. The kids began to snicker quite a bit. The mother wondered what was up with the kids. She soon figured out what was going on as both of the young ladies, alternately, bent over wearing skirts that were far too short.

The two young ladies were both wearing thong's that exposed a little too much. Appalled, the mother took the kids to a different area. It didn't seem to matter what section of the store the mother and her kids would move to; they would eventually run into the same two young ladies as they continued their behavior time after time.

Finally, the mother had had enough. She went to the manager to voice her complaint. The manager came and asked the young ladies to leave the store, but they refused. The manager called the cops. The cops arrived and talked to the young ladies about such things as indecent exposure and disorderly conduct. The cops gave the young ladies an ultimatum. Either buy something decent to cover themselves, or receive a physical administration of the W.A.L., followed by a trip downtown. The ladies chose to buy appropriate garments, put them on, and leave the store.

Frank's Lesson

About every other day, for the past couple of weeks, Frank had been receiving a very painful attitude adjustment, administered by the few members of Bobby's team who stayed in town for a while to encourage him to do the right thing. One of the guys told Frank, "The time has come to set you free, that is… from our custody. Now here's what will happen. We're gonna drop you off a few blocks from a certain precinct. You are instructed to walk up to that precinct and turn yourself in. Now, along the way… I'm sure that the thought to run will come to mind. Just know this… should you decide to run… it's only gonna land you right back here in our custody. And believe me… you don't want that!"

Frank was dropped off at a designated spot. Under very specific instructions, he walked up to the police station to turn himself in. After spending the last few weeks in the custody of a few of Bobby's team members, who elected to stay and show him what his life would be like, if he did not turn himself in, Frank decided that he would much rather go to prison than remain in the custody of those guys.

In The News

The word was out. It's been duly noted that the W.A.L. is here, and it appears to be working quite well. It had become common knowledge that the W.A.L. was not confined to any specific type of crime. The Whoop-Ass-Law applies to broken laws in general. As for all who actually received a physical application, of the W.A.L., none were repeat offenders of the same sort.

On Saturday, at a large warehouse on the south side of town, police held a no questions asked weapons buyback program. People were lined up almost as if they were attending a concert or some type of sporting event.

Gun surrender programs had been held many times in the past. But this, by far, was the most successful ever to be recorded anywhere in the nation.

CHAPTER
28

Final trip to Indy

Offer on The Cross Property

After about ten weeks had gone by, Toni, from A-1 Realty, made a call to Lee, who was now back in California at the studio. As they had just rapped a set and were leaving, his cell phone began to ring. Noticing the number as being that of the realtor's office, he answered the phone, "Hey, Toni!" Remembering the mix up from a previous call he said, "Or Karen?"

Toni responded "No, it's Toni, you got it right the first time."

"Good," he said, "I should be more careful with that."

"I hope I didn't catch you at a bad time," Toni said.

"No time is a bad time to hear from you, especially if you have good news," Lee responded.

"As a matter of fact, I believe I do," Toni said, "I have an offer on your property." She shared the numbers with Lee.

"Well now," Lee said, "that certainly is good news, and it couldn't have come at a better time. It just so happens… I have a meeting scheduled with your good mayor on Monday. I can stop by your office after the meeting to get everything finalized."

"Great!" I shall look forward to it. See you then, and good luck with the mayor!"

Lee Meets Lindsey

Lee returned to Indianapolis on Sunday afternoon. The first stop he made even before going to check on his property, was to pay a visit to Michelle. He rang the doorbell upon arrival. As the door opened, he expected to see the face of Michelle, but instead, it was Lindsey answering the door, "Yes, may I help you?"

"And you must be Lindsey," Lee said.

Lindsey was shocked to discover a gentleman at the door that she did not recognize, but who seemed to know of her.

"Yes, I am. Should I know you, or--"

"Oh, I'm sorry, please forgive me! I'm Lee… Leander Cross. I've been working with your mother on some, uh, well, I guess you might say political issues." Lindsey lit up, "Oh Yeah! Of course, Lee! I've heard quite a bit about you. Please, come in and have a seat. I'll get mom!"

Lindsey went to find Michelle, calling out along the way, "Mom… oh mother dear… you have company." She found her mom and beckoned her into the living room. Michelle was pleasantly surprised to find Lee, there, sitting on the sofa. The two greeted one another with a rather intense hug. "Well, I guess you've met my daughter, Lindsey. Lindsey, this is Mr. Cross."

"You mean Lee, your... political partner." Lindsey said with a handshake, "So nice to finally meet you, Mr. Cross."

Both Lee and Michelle were fully aware that Lindsey was just poking fun at them.

"I understand you've been away on a college tour. So how was it," Lee asked?

"It was great! A lot of my friends were there. This year, for the first time, they included a camping trip. I thought that was a nice touch. It provided a fun atmosphere and a chance for potential students to come together and share their thoughts about attending in the fall. Yeah, it was pretty great alright, not to mention, all of the cute guys there as well. But that will have no bearing on my decision as to whether or not I will attend there."

Lindsey just couldn't leave without poking a little more fun at the two of them.

"The only thing that bothered me while I was away, was the thought of my mother being here all alone, possibly, feeling sad and lonely."

Again, both Lee and Michelle were fully aware that Lindsey was just poking fun at them.

"Well, just as a good mother would be, I'm sure she was plenty worried about you as well," Lee said.

"Uh huh... well, anyway... it was nice to meet you, Mr. Cross. Well, I'm off to the mall now. So, I guess I'll just leave you two alone to discuss your... politics." Lee and Michelle could only smile at one another as Lindsey left.

After Lindsey had gone, the two made small talk for a bit. Michelle was surprised to learn that Lee had made his first stop there, to see her, even before going to check on his own place. Lee mentioned his upcoming meeting with the mayor, and he also informed her that his realtor had found a buyer for his property.

Later in the evening, Lindsey returned from the mall, and Lee was gone. She found her mom in the kitchen.

"I see you let him get away, huh!" Lindsey said.

"Excuse me?"

"Oh mom," Lindsey said, "You know he's cute!"

"Well, I--"

"Just admit it, mom," Lindsey said, "the guy is fine, okay? And it's soooo obvious that politics is not the only common denominator here. But it's okay though... You deserve to have a life!"

"Now, listen to little miss cupid! Maybe you just need to chill on all of that, okay?"

"Alright! But I'm just saying..."

Changing the subject, Michelle asked, "So anyway... what did you buy at the mall?" Lindsey showed her mom the purchases she had made. And the two of them enjoyed the rest of their evening at home.

Final Meeting with The Mayor

Early Monday morning, Lee went to meet with the mayor. Upon arrival, he was greeted by the receptionist who shook his hand and showed him to the mayor's office. She opened the door and presented him to the mayor. "Mr. Cross is here to see you, Sir!"

The mayor responded cheerfully, "Mr. Cross! Come in Sir! Please... sit! You know... I have a little confession to make. When you first came to us with this whole idea about gun control and the W.A.L., I thought... man this guy must be crazy if he thinks for one minute, that any of this will work, or even so, that people would go for it. And perhaps, I'd be even crazier to give it any kind of consideration. But I gotta tell ya... the more you talked, and the more I listened... the more it started to make sense."

"Well, Mr. Mayor... I'm very happy to hear that!"

"You know... I've been in and around politics for nearly my entire adult life. And I can honestly say... that I can't ever recall an idea that became a bill, and got passed, as quickly as this one," The Mayor said.

"It was pretty fast!" Lee responded.

"Obviously, there's a lot of people out there who feel the same as you and I about putting a stop to all of these senseless murders. But it would take someone with, uh... well, let's say... very large cojones, to bring such an idea to the forefront," the mayor said.

"Thing is..." Lee said, "people are tired of a bunch of strong words followed by soft actions. They're ready for a change, you know? Real change! Not just strong words... but strong actions as well. They want actions that get results."

"And speaking of results," the mayor said, "since the initiation of the W.A.L., coupled with a few demonstrations from law enforcement, in just a few short weeks, we've already seen a huge reduction in crime. I'm talking crimes such as home invasions, armed robbery, carjacking, homicide, rape, and trafficking. Calls reporting a nuisance... down! Indecent exposure... down! I mean, you name it, all the numbers are down. I'm talking about a drastic decline in crimes, all across the board. And that, my friend... is what I call results.

This new law has also allowed us to confiscate a lot more contraband than in times past. But the part that pleases me, is that as news of the W.A.L. spreads throughout the city, our no questions asked, weapons surrender program, is seeing record numbers of volunteer gun surrendering. Just this past Saturday, it was reported that a very large number of people were lined up to turn in their guns. It looked as if they were waiting to get into a concert. It was by far, the largest turnout the nation has ever seen for this type of event. Looks as though a lot of criminals, or would-be criminals, would prefer not to have the W.A.L. come down on them.

On that same Saturday, while the police conducted the weapons buyback program, we also experienced another record turnout. A large gathering of MOMS PLUS, which consist of not only moms, but all who support them as well, came and filled monument circle.

They were there as a showing of solidarity in favor of the new Gunsmart System, that would make America a Gunsmart Nation."

"Great," Lee said, "Together, I know we can stop the violence!"

"Oh yeah... and one more thing," the mayor added, "It just may interest you to know that the guy who organized that little fiasco at your place... we now have in custody."

"Well, that certainly is good news. Glad to hear it!"

"Yeah, it certainly is," the mayor said, "but the weirdest thing... I don't believe I've ever heard of a guy of his caliber, to all of a sudden... just up and turn himself in. It seemed as if he felt he'd be better off in police custody versus being out on the street."

"Huh... well how about that!"

"Yeah," the mayor repeated, "how about that. You know... I can't help but wonder... if the W.A.L. may have played a part in that?"

"Well, what can I say... I guess that just goes to show that anything's possible, huh? But one thing's for certain... the W.A.L. serves as an absolute deterrent for anyone who may be considering criminal behavior. If I've said it once... I've said it a thousand times... the W.A.L. works!"

"You're right about that," the mayor said, "Yes sir... you are right about that!"

The mayor asked, "Can I offer you something to drink, coffee, water, or anything?"

"No, I'm good, thanks." Lee went on to share his thoughts on part two of the W.A.L.

Closing the Deal

Lee visited the realtor's office, where he sat down with the owner, Toni Bradshaw, to complete the sale of the property. He signed a stack of papers and handed them back to Toni. She escorted him out to the lobby where she handed the paperwork to Karen.

"Well, I guess this finishes our business.

It's been a pleasure dealing with you, and I certainly thank you for such a great service," Lee said.

"You're quite welcome," Toni responded, "and believe me... the pleasure was all mine. I do hope that you're satisfied with the numbers."

"Very much so! Well, I gotta run now." He handed her his business card. "But if you're ever in the Hollywood area, please give me a call. Perhaps I could show you some kind of appreciation for all of your wonderful help."

"Well, I'll certainly keep that in mind," Toni said.

Karen was watching and taking it all in, as Lee and Toni said their goodbyes. She rolled her eyes as she said under her breath, "Yeah, and I guess I'll certainly be calling American Airlines to book you a flight."

"Well, you ladies have a great day, and uh... perhaps, we'll meet again sometime."

"Perhaps!" Toni said. Neither Lee nor Toni noticed Karen as she mocked the two of them by making a gagging motion.

"Bye now!" Lee said to the ladies.

As he turned to walk out, both, Toni and Karen, responded simultaneously, "Byyyeee!"

Toni started to head back to her office when she received a playful, smart remark from Karen, "Oh, why don't you two just get a room already... and save yourself a trip!" Toni, also responding playfully, "Oh shut up and get back to work!"

The Final Goodbye

Michelle drove by the Cross property on her way home. She noticed a person putting a sign in the yard, that read, SOLD! She continued home where she pulled into the garage and lowered the door. She entered the kitchen and sat her bags on the bar. She took out her cell phone and listened to messages while pouring a drink from the fridge. She thumbed through some mail. The doorbell rang just as she was about to take a drink. She set the glass down and went to answer the door.

Once again, Michelle was happy to find Lee, standing at the door.

"Well, what a pleasant surprise," She said, "Come in! I was just about to have some lemonade. Come… join me!" They returned to the kitchen, where Michelle poured another glass of lemonade and handed it to Lee.

"Thank you," he said.

"I saw the SOLD sign in the yard, as I passed by your place, just a little while ago, as I was on my way home."

"Yeah… I… uh… I just left the realtor's office," Lee said. Michelle responded rather softly, "I see!"

The normal cheerfulness that was usually shared between the two of them was now starting to dissipate. They had become slow to respond to one another's comments. The volume at which they now spoke had lowered significantly. It was obvious, one to the other, that they both were experiencing a bit of sadness, as goodbye was becoming apparent. This was the moment they both realize that they had developed feelings for one another. Softly spoken, Michelle said, "Well, it looks as though, you're all done here… and this is goodbye."

"I suppose it is," he said.

There was a moment of silence.

"I have a car waiting, so, I guess I'd better…"

"Yes, I… I understand," Michelle said.

They head out front where the driver waited to take Lee to the airport.

Standing just outside of the front door, they shared a rather passionate and lengthy embrace. After their bodies separated, they continued to hold hands a little while longer as they said their final goodbyes.

"I wanna thank you for all of your help. And I really appreciate your bringing forth such great ideas. All across America, millions of MOMS are speaking out, in favor of the new Gunsmart System that could make America a Gunsmart Nation. I couldn't have done it without you. And I know that Paula would be well pleased. Again, thank you so much!" Michelle said.

"You're quite welcome... and the pleasure was all mine. I enjoyed working with you. So, this is goodbye for now. But honestly... it doesn't feel very good at all, to me! But remember, there is still work to be done on the national level. After Carrington gets those meetings set up, in the areas that he refers to as the nations' hot spots, we shall meet again.

You know... I believe it's the book of Ecclesiastes that let us know that things are not always as we think. Being my dad's power of attorney, I thought I'd come here only to sell the house. Little did I know that I would team up with someone, to become an advocate for gun control, and accomplish all that we have. And even more surprising... is that I would meet, such a beautiful lady... one that I could so easily see myself falling for." He continued, "Well, I guess I'd better not keep the driver waiting much longer. He might just decide to leave me."

Lee released Michelle's hand as he turned to face the car.

"Well, If the driver should happen to leave you... one more night spent here wouldn't be so bad now, would It?" Michelle asked.

Still facing the car, Lee responded, "Actually, I imagine it would be quite good. Really good! Perhaps... too good!"

"Why are you talking with your back to me?" she asked. Lee replied, "As hard as it is to leave... I really must go. But if I turn to look back at you once more... I'm not so sure that I'll be able to leave. And I really must go!"

Slowly, he started walking toward the car. Michelle wanted to stop him, and almost dose. But she restrained herself, as she realized that, his life was Hollywood, and hers was Indy. Michelle watched him as he got into the car and shut the door. The car pulled off. Lee never looked back. She was left staring as the car disappeared out of sight.

Michelle returned to the kitchen. She sat on a bar stool, slowly stirring her lemonade with a straw. She got full of emotions, and ran to the front door, hoping to find Lee standing there just one more time.

She opened the door but found no one there. Once again, Michelle stood in the doorway, staring at the spot where the car disappeared from her sight. Realizing that he was really gone, she slowly shut the door.

Epilogue

This work of fiction is indeed inspired by, but not based on, actual occurrences. The focus of this book is to shine a light on a longstanding problem that continues to plague our nation. The intent is to offer a solution to the problem.

The solution has now been revealed, and the ball is now in The People's court.

The two main characters in this story, Lee and Michelle, though they live in different parts of the country and talks between them have slowed, will continue to push for greater gun control.

IN THE BOOK THAT FOLLOWS

Several months go by before Congressman Andre Carrington sets-up a gun reform meeting in Los Angeles. Lee expected to reunite with Michelle during her visit. But what he did not expect was to see both Sasha Gaines and Toni Bradshaw who were also in town for a realtors' conference. Three ladies desiring the attention of one man. It's going to be an interesting weekend in L. A.

ABOUT THE AUTHOR

Highest among his earlier set of dreams, and aspirations, were his dreams to become a professional football player. He dreamt that, as a running back for the Dallas Cowboys, wearing his favorite number twenty-two, he would someday go on to break all kinds of NFL records.

Dwight's idol was, wide receiver, Bob Hayes. There was a time when Hayes was considered the fastest man in the world. As speed was Dwight's ace in the hole, he thought that one day he would hold that title. He believed that someday he would go on to win the Super Bowl and receive the MVP Award.

Growing up, he played football in Indiana and Mississippi. Dwight possessed a vast amount of speed, peripheral vision, agility, and strength, all of which served him well. No one could have ever told him that he would not have a great career in the NFL.

Unfortunately, he let his abilities go to his head. One day he made a dumb decision, in defiance of the coach's authority, which ultimately led to him being let go from the team. Never in his life had he ever experienced such hurt as the day that he had to turn in his uniform. He felt as though a part of him died. Of course, he figured he would just go someplace else and put the pieces back together again. Instead, he just kept running into one hurdle after another.

So, the years passed, and finally, he realized that this particular dream was never going to become a reality. He came to accept the fact that this was not God's will for his life. Even so, giving up on his dream still hurt a lot.

Dwight shied away from football, for a long time, because he couldn't stand to watch. After several years had gone by, along comes a running back wearing number twenty-two for the Dallas Cowboys. This guy went on to win the Super Bowl and receive the MVP award. He's a great player and a great guy.

Dwight became a big fan of the guy and was very happy for him and all of his achievements. But honestly, he couldn't help but think, "Wow! That was supposed to be my story!"

Aside from the sports that he participated in, which were Football, Basketball, Track, and Boxing, at an early age, Dwight also took a liking to the arts. He enjoyed music, drawing, and writing. His mindset, at the time, was such that the arts would always come second to sports. Little did he know... writing would be the thing that he would become most passionate about.

Here, he has written about some very strong, and possible, solutions to the gun violence that plagues our nation. How could anyone ever disagree with the life-saving solutions that are revealed within the pages of this book?

www.ingramcontent.com/pod-product-compliance
Lightning Source LLC
Chambersburg PA
CBHW031512270326
41930CB00006B/368

* 9 7 8 1 7 3 3 6 5 0 2 4 3 *